TESTIMONY OF THE HOLY QURAN

Regarding the Advent of the Promised Messiah in the Latter Days

Testimony of the Holy Quran

Regarding the Advent of the Promised Messiah in the Latter Days

(Shahādatul-Qur'ān
'alā nuzūlil-masīḥil-mau'ūd
fī ākhiriz-zamān)

Ḥaḍrat Mirza Ghulam Ahmad

The Promised Messiah and Mahdi[as],
Founder of the Ahmadiyya Muslim Community

ISLAM INTERNATIONAL PUBLICATIONS LTD.

ISLAM INTERNATIONAL PUBLICATIONS LTD

Testimony of the Holy Quran
Regarding the Advent of the
Promised Messiah in the Latter Days
(*Shahādatul-Qur'ān 'alā nuzūlil-masīḥil-mau'ūd*
fī ākhiriz-zamān)

By Ḥaḍrat Mirza Ghulam Ahmad
The Promised Messiah and Mahdi, peace be on him,
Founder of the Ahmadiyya Muslim Community

First published in Urdu in Qadian, India, 1893
First English translation published in the UK, 2021

Published by
Islam International Publications Ltd.
Unit 3, Bourne Mill Business Park,
Guildford Road, Farnham,
Surrey, UK. GU9 9PS

For further information please visit www.alislam.org

Cover design by: Usman Nasir Choudhary

ISBN: 978-1-84880-570-5
10 9 8 7 6 5 4 3 2 1

CONTENTS

Ḥaḍrat Mirza Ghulam Ahmad of Qadian

The Promised Messiah & Mahdi [as]

ABOUT THE AUTHOR

Ḥaḍrat Mirza Ghulam Ahmad[as] was born in 1835 in Qadian, India. From his early life, he dedicated himself to prayer, and the study of the Holy Quran and other scriptures. He was deeply pained to observe the plight of Islam, which was being attacked from all directions. In order to defend Islam and present its teachings in their pristine purity, he wrote more than ninety books, thousands of letters, and participated in many religious debates. He argued that Islam is a living faith, which can lead man to establish communion with God and achieve moral and spiritual perfection.

Ḥaḍrat Mirza Ghulam Ahmad[as] started experiencing divine dreams, visions, and revelations at a young age. In 1889, under divine command, he started accepting initiation into the Ahmadiyya Muslim Community. The divine revelations continued to increase and he was commanded by God to announce that God had appointed him to be the same Reformer of the Latter Days as prophesied by various religions under different titles. He claimed to be the same Promised Messiah and Mahdi whose advent had been prophesied by the Holy Prophet Muḥammad[sas].

The Ahmadiyya Muslim Community is now established in more than 200 countries.

After his demise in 1908, the institution of *Khilāfat* (successorship) was established to succeed him, in fulfilment of the prophecies made in the Holy Quran and by the Holy Prophet Muḥammad[sas]. Ḥaḍrat Mirza Masroor Ahmad[aba] is the Fifth Successor to the Promised Messiah[as] and the present head of the Ahmadiyya Muslim Community.

FOREWORD

In *Shahādatul Qur'ān,* Ḥaḍrat Mirza Ghulam Ahmad[as] addresses a number of fundamental questions raised by a gentleman named Ata Muhammad concerning the advent of the Promised Messiah in Islam. Thes questions include:

- If the Promised Messiah's advent is prophesied only in the Hadith, are such *aḥādīth* reliable?
- Does the Holy Quran speak of the Promised Messiah's advent?
- Assuming the prophecies are true, what proof is there that they were fulfilled in the person of Ḥaḍrat Mirza Ghulam Ahmad[as]?

In dealing with these questions, the author first clarifies the lofty status of the Hadith and emphasizes their importance as a fundamental source of Islamic history, the life of the Holy Prophet[ṣas], and knowledge regarding Islamic worship and commandments. He concludes: It is necessary to accept what is stated in the Hadith unless the Quran contradicts it in clear and explicit terms.

With regard to the prophecies relating to the Promised Messiah, the author asserts that the strength and continuity of narration of the *aḥādīth* on this subject, as well as the multiplicity of Islamic books which record it, leave no doubt concerning their authenticity.

Turning to the Holy Quran, the author demonstrates that several prophecies contained in its verses, regarding the Latter Days, have come to pass. It follows, then, that the intertwined prophecies concerning the Messiah should also be fulfilled.

The very fact that the author is the only such claimant upon the fulfilment of the prophecies of the Latter Days, stands as a testimony to his truthfulness; moreover, he argues that he is supported by Signs of God in the way all Prophets had been supported before him. He invites Ata Muhammad to ask that a Sign be manifested about him. The latter, however, chose not to pursue this matter any further.

A study of this book will be certainly beneficial to those who want to understand the truthfulness of the Promised Messiah according to the Holy Quran and Hadith.

Al-Ḥāj Munir-ud-Din Shams
Additional Wakīlut-Taṣnīf, London
July 2021

Testimony of the Holy Quran

الحمد للہ والمنت کہ رسالہ طیبہ مبارکہ

المسماۃ بہ

شہادۃ القرآن علی نزول المسیح الموعود فی آخر الزمان

مطبع پنجاب پریس سیالکوٹ میں باہتمام

منشی غلام قادر صاحب

فصیح کے چھپا

قیمت (۶/)

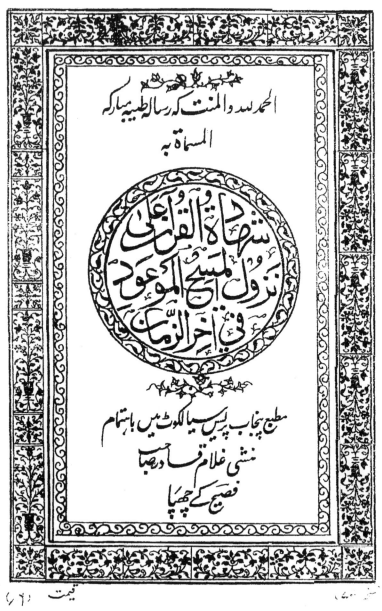

Facsimile of the original title page for *Shahādatul-Qur'ān* printed in 1893.

GOD BE PRAISED AND THANKED
FOR THE PUBLICATION OF THIS BOOKLET

Testimony of the Holy Quran

Regarding the Advent of the Promised Messiah in the Latter Days

PRINTED AT THE PUNJAB PRESS, SIALKOT;

under the supervision of
Munshi Ghulam Qādir Faṣīḥ

COPIES 700 PRICE SIX ANNA

Translation of the original title page for *Shahādatul-Qur'ān*.

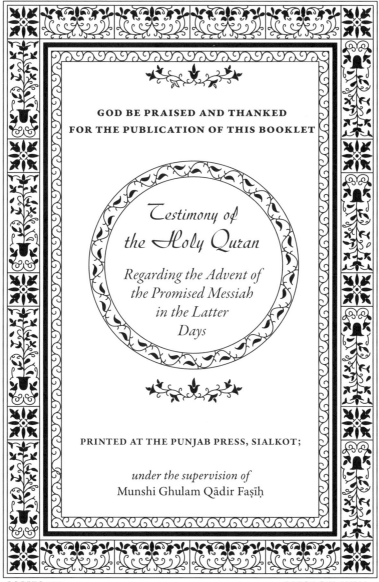

اشتہار کتب

اس وقت جو

اس عاجز کی تالیفات میں سے

کتابیں موجود ہیں ان کی تفصیل حسب ذیل ہے۔

حصہ چہارم براہین احمدیہ .... للعہ ر

سرمہ چشم آریہ .... عمار

فتح اسلام ۳ر

توضیح مرام ۴ر

ازالہ اوہام .... سے ر

آئینہ کمالات اسلام .... عمار

تفسیر سورۃ ☆ الفاتحہ معہ قصائد بزبان عربی ۶ر

تحفہ بغداد بزبان عربی ۳ر

برکات الدعاء ۴ر

محصول ڈاک علاوہ

المشتہر

خاکسار

غلام احمد قادیانی

☆ اس تفسیر کے ساتھ ایک ہزار روپیہ کا انعام ان علماء کے لئے جو اس کی نظیر بنا سکیں۔

Facsimile of the original Urdu Announcement page in *Shahādatul-Qur'ān*

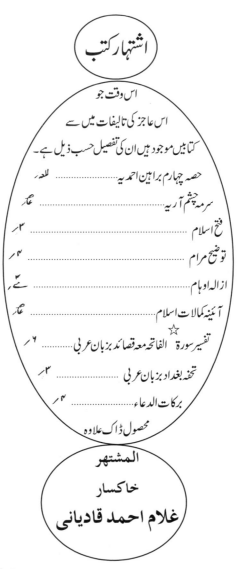

ADVERTISEMENT OF BOOKS

At present, of the books written by this humble one, the ones available are listed below

Barāhīn-e-Aḥmadiyya, Part IV..................................*Rs. 4*

Surmah Chashm-e-Āryah [*Guidance for the Aryas*]...*Rs. 2*

Fatḥ-e- Islām [*Victory of Islam*]............................ *3 Annas*

Tauḍīḥ-e-Marām [*Elucidation of Objectives*]....... *4 Annas*

Izāla-e-Auhām [*The Removal of Misconceptions*].......*Rs. 3*

Ā'īna-e-Kamālāt-e-Islām
[*The Mirror of the Excellences of Islam*].......................*Rs. 2*

Tafsīr Sūrah☆ *al-Fātiḥah ma'a Qaṣa'id bazubān Arabī*
[*Commentary of Surah al-Fatihah, with Odes in Arabic*]...
.... *6 Annas*

Tuḥfa-e-Baghdād bazubān Arabī
[*A Gift for Baghdad in Arabic*] .... *3 Annas*

Barakātud-Du'ā' [*The Blessings of Prayer*]........... *4 Annas*

POSTAGE ADDITIONAL

Published by
the humble one,
GHULAM AHMAD OF QADIAN

☆ This commentary comes with prize of Rs. 1,000 for those ulema who can produce its equal.

Translation of the original Urdu Announcement page in *Shahādatul-Qur'ān*

بِسۡمِ اللّٰهِ الرَّحۡمٰنِ الرَّحِيۡمِ [1]

اَلۡحَمۡدُ لِلّٰهِ وَالسَّلَامُ عَلٰى عِبَادِهِ الَّذِيۡنَ اصۡطَفٰى [2]

The Promised Messiah

A gentleman named ʿAṭā Muhammad enquires of me through his letter, published in August 1893, as to what is the proof of my being the Promised Messiah and whether we are obliged and duty-bound to wait for any messiah.

In this context, we must first bear in mind that the critic holds the belief that Ḥaḍrat ʿĪsā [Jesus], peace be upon him, has indeed died, as is mentioned clearly in the Holy Quran. But he denies that someone bearing the name of ʿĪsā will appear in this ummah. He accepts that *aḥādīth* [pl. hadith] do, indeed, record this prophecy, but considers the reports of such *aḥādīth* to be unreliable. He argues that the *aḥādīth* were collected after a long period and most of them are *aḥād* [solitary traditions, not

1. In the name of Allah, the Gracious, the Merciful. [Publisher]
2. Allah be praised, and blessings be on his chosen servants. [Publisher]

supported by others] therefore, they lack certainty. That is why he does not regard the prophecy about the Promised Messiah, which is confirmed by *aḥādīth,* as an established fact. In his view, prophecies based on *aḥādīth* alone are worthless and unfounded and, therefore, cannot qualify as substantial proof. So, it seems necessary that I answer his queries in keeping with his way of thinking. Let it be clear that in this matter there are three issues calling for investigation:

> **FIRST:** Whether the prophecy regarding the advent of the Promised Messiah, which is recorded in the *aḥādīth,* is unreliable because the accounts of *aḥādīth* are far from and entirely outside the level of certainty;
> **SECOND:** Whether or not this prophecy finds any mention in the Holy Quran;
> **THIRD:** If this prophecy is a proven fact, what proof, then, is there that it has been fulfilled in the person of my humble self?

Let me begin with addressing the **FIRST OF THESE THREE ISSUES.** Let it be clear that no one denies that the *aḥādīth* contain an explicit prophecy about the Promised Messiah. Rather, there is a consensus among almost all the Muslims that, as per *aḥādīth,* a person is sure to come who will be named ʻĪsā ibn Maryam [Jesus Son of Mary]. And this prophecy finds such repeated mention in the books of Hadith—*Bukhārī*, *Muslim*, *Tirmidhī*, etc.—that it is enough to satisfy a fair-minded person and compels us to believe in their common theme that a Promised Messiah is to come. It is true that most such *aḥādīth,* taken individually, are no more than *aḥād,* yet it cannot be denied that all the *aḥādīth,* assembled from various sources regarding this issue, when collectively examined, establish categorically and conclusively that the Holy Prophet, peace and blessings of Allah be upon him, has certainly prophesied the advent of the Promised Messiah. Moreover, when we read the *aḥādīth* possessed by *Ahl-e-Sunnat wal-Jamā'at*, along with those *aḥādīth* on which other sects of Islam, such as Shias, rely, the strength of such *aḥādīth* having *tawātur* [multiple narrators] is even more firmly established. Additionally, hundreds of books of the sufis also testify to this fact. And when we consult the literature of the People of the Book, that is, the Christians, we find this prophecy in their books as well.

The verdict of Ḥaḍrat Masīḥ[as] [Jesus] in the Gospels regarding the descent of Ilyās [Elijah] from heaven demonstrates that such prophecies can never be taken literally. However, the prophecy about the advent of the Promised Messiah appears so extensively in every age that it would be gross ignorance to deny that it possesses *tawātur*. I say truthfully that if all Islamic books in which this prophecy is recorded were to be collected in chronological order, their number would definitely run into the thousands. But it is difficult to make someone understand who is unfamiliar with the corpus of Islamic literature. In fact, such critics are unfortunately so ignorant that they simply do not understand how strongly and forcefully the veracity of a certain event is established.

This critic simply heard from someone that most of the *aḥādīth* are at the level of *aḥād* and he has immediately concluded that, with the exception of the Holy Quran, all other authorities in Islam are baseless and doubtful and are completely devoid of certainty and conclusiveness. But in reality, this is a great mistake, the first result of which is to destroy faith and religion. If it were true that with the exception of the Holy Quran all other documentary sources are a bundle of falsehood, imposture, deceit, conjectures, and imagination, then, perhaps only a little would be left of Islam; for all the details of our Faith have come down to us through the *aḥādīth* of the Holy Prophet[sas]. For example, the requirement of the formal Prayer—which we offer five times a day—is established by the Holy Quran, but nowhere does the Quran lay down that the morning Prayer comprises two obligatory *rak'āt* [units of Prayer] and two *rak'āt* of *sunnah; Ḍhuhr* [Prayer] comprises four *rak'āt* of *farḍ* and four and two *rak'āt* of *sunnah; Maghrib* [Prayer]comprises three *rak'āt* of *farḍ;* and *'Ishā'* [Prayer] comprises four *rak'āt*. In the same way, we have to depend entirely upon *aḥādīth* to learn the details of zakat.

Moreover, there are thousands of details relating to worship, dealings, covenants, and so on; they are so well known that writing about them would be a waste of time and needless prolongation. Besides, the primary and principal source of Islamic history is *aḥādīth*. If the reports contained in *aḥādīth* are not relied upon, then we should also not take it as certain that Ḥaḍrat Abū Bakr, Ḥaḍrat 'Umar, Ḥaḍrat Uthmān, and Ḥaḍrat 'Alī, may Allah be pleased with them, were the Companions of the Holy Prophet, peace and blessings of Allah be upon him, who became the *Khulafā'* [successors] of the Holy Prophet, peace and blessings of Allah be upon him, in this order and also died in this order. If the accounts related by *aḥādīth* are not trusted, there would be no reason to believe with certainty in the existence of these great personalities. It might be possible to infer that all these names are fictitious and that there was no Abū Bakr, no 'Umar, no Uthmān, and no Ali; for, according to our critic, Miyāṅ Ata Muhammad, all these *aḥādīth* are *aḥād* and the Holy Quran nowhere mentions these names, so how can these *aḥādīth* be considered authentic in light of this principle.

In the same way, shall we deny that the name of the father of the Holy Prophet, peace and blessings of Allah be upon him, was 'Abdullah, and his mother's name was Āminah; and the name of his grandfather was 'Abdul Muṭṭalib and one of his wives was named Khadījah and another 'Ā'ishah, and another Ḥafṣah, may Allah be pleased with them; and that the name of his wet-nurse was Ḥalimah; and that the Holy Prophet, peace and blessings of Allah be on him, used to withdraw to the Cave of Hira for worship; and that some of his Companions migrated to Abyssinia; and that for ten years after his advent, the Holy Prophet, peace and blessings of Allah be upon him, resided in Makkah. Moreover, there were all those battles that the Noble Quran does not even mention. All these matters are established by *aḥādīth* alone. Can we deny the occurrence of all these events on the alleged basis that *aḥādīth* amount to nothing?

Were that so, it would not be possible for the Muslims to relate any portion of the biography of the Holy Prophet, peace and blessings of Allah be upon him. It should be observed that the events of the life of our lord and master, the kind of life he led in Makkah before his advent, the year he called people to his Prophethood, the order in which people embraced Islam, how the disbelievers persecuted them in the ten years in Makkah, how and why battles began, and in which of them the blessed person of the Holy Prophet, peace and blessings of Allah be upon him, himself took part, and to which regions the rule of Islam had extended in the lifetime of his holy and honoured personage, and whether the Holy Prophet, peace and blessings of Allah be on him, addressed letters to the rulers of the time, inviting them to Islam, and if he did so, what was the result, and after the death of the Holy Prophet, peace and blessings of Allah be on him, what were the victories achieved during the time of Ḥaḍrat Abū Bakr Ṣiddīq, and what difficulties came about, and in the time of Ḥaḍrat [ʻUmar] Fārūq which countries did Islam achieve conquests—all these matters are known only through *aḥādīth* and the statements of the Companions. Hence, if *aḥādīth* amount to nothing, it would not just be difficult, but rather quite impossible, to learn of the events of that time, and in such a case the opponents of Islam would be free to invent whatever lies they like concerning the events of the life of the Holy Prophet, peace and blessings of Allah be upon him, and of the lives of his Companions, may Allah be pleased with them. We would thus provide to the enemies of Islam a great opportunity to make baseless attacks against Islam, and we would have to admit that all the events and incidents related in *aḥādīth* are baseless and imaginary, so much so that even the names of the Companions are not known with certainty. To suppose that we cannot derive any certain and conclusive truth from *aḥādīth* amounts to destroying a great portion of Islam with our own hands.

The true and correct position is that it is necessary to accept what is stated in the *aḥādīth* unless the Quran contradicts it in clear and explicit terms. For, it is established that it is natural for man to tell the truth and that he resorts to falsehood under some compulsion, for falsehood is unnatural for him. Therefore, doubting the conclusiveness and reliability of those *aḥādīth* that had—through becoming a consistent practice or collective belief—developed into a characteristic of different groups of Muslims, is really a type of insanity and madness. For instance, if anyone were to contend that the number of *rak'āt* the Muslims perform in the five daily prayers is a doubtful matter, inasmuch as there is no verse in the Holy Quran prescribing two *rak'āt* for the morning Prayer and two for *Jumu'ah,* and two each for the two Eid prayers, and that most *aḥādīth* are *aḥād* and thus unreliable, would such a one be in the right? If such views were accepted about the *aḥādīth,* then the first thing to be lost would be prayer itself, for the Holy Quran has nowhere prescribed the method of offering prayers; rather, they are offered only on the basis of our reliance that the [relevant] *aḥādīth* are correct.

Now, if an opponent raises the objection that the Holy Quran does not teach how to offer prayer and the way the Muslims have adopted for offering prayer is to be rejected because the *aḥādīth* are unreliable—and if we, too, adhere to the same principle, that the *aḥādīth* are worthless—how could we respond to this objection, except to accept it? Indeed in such a case, Islam's funeral prayer would also become utterly futile, because nowhere does the Holy Quran mention any prayer without prostration and bowing. Now ponder and see what is left of Islam if the *aḥādīth* are discarded.

Besides, the very notion that the sayings of the Messenger of Allah, peace and blessings of Allah be upon him, are considered authentic merely because of the supposed authenticity of the reports of one or two narrators is a matter resulting from a lack of reflection. The fact is that the *aḥādīth* constitute a branch of the *ta'āmul* [continued practice] and were collected and compiled after those practices became established. For example, the *muḥaddithīn* [hadith scholars] observed that millions of people offer three *rak'āt* of *farḍ* in *Maghrib,* and two in *Fajr,* and always recite *Sūrah al-Fātiḥah* in every *rak'at,* and say *āmīn* either loudly or silently. Likewise, they observed them offering [supplications like] *at-taḥiyyāt, durūd,* and many prayers in the last sitting position, and concluding their Prayer by offering *salām* to their right and left. Seeing this manner of worship, the *muḥaddithīn* became eager and interested to verify this matter by tracing this method of prayer back to the Holy Prophet, peace and blessings of Allah be on him and to confirm it through *aḥādīth* that are *ṣaḥīḥ* [authentic], and *marfū'* and *muttaṣil* [i.e. whose chains of narration reach up to the Holy Prophet[sas] and are uninterrupted].

It is true that the *muḥaddithīn* have not provided chains of a thousand or two thousand narrators for every single hadith. But would it be right to assume that it was the *muḥaddithīn* who established prayer in the first place, and before them people did not offer prayer and were totally unaware of it, and that it was only after many centuries that people, relying on one or two *aḥādīth,* began to offer prayer? Hence, I declare emphatically that it would be a grave misconception to believe that the manner and *rak'āt* of prayer were proven solely on the basis of a handful of *aḥādīth* that appear to be *aḥād.* If that were to be true, then, first of all, Islamic observances would suffer an irremediable setback—which would be of grave concern for any Muslim with a sense of honour. But remember that only those people labour under such misconceptions who have never attentively studied Islamic chronicles, history, traditions, rites, and worship, and who are unaware of how and with what process these matters were authenticated.

Let it be clear that the continuous practice of people establishes the certainty of these matters with utmost satisfaction. For example, let us suppose that there are only two or three such *aḥādīth* which relate that the number of *rak'āt* in the *Fajr* Prayer is X and the *rak'āt* in the *Maghrib* prayer is Y, and it is granted that these *aḥādīth* are no more than *aḥād*. Now, did the people not offer the prayer prior to this research and investigation? Was it only after authenticating the *aḥādīth* and learning of their narrators that the daily prayers were initiated? Nay, millions of people offered prayer in the prescribed way. Let us assume that the study of the chain of narrators of *aḥādīth* had not even existed, even then the continuous practice would definitively and categorically have established that Islamic teachings regarding prayer has remained the same generation after generation, and century after century. The existence of uninterrupted chains of narrators culminating with the Holy Prophet[sas] serves to reinforce the continuous practice. In light of this principle, it would be an egregious mistake to pronounce most of the *aḥādīth*—which are corroborated and supported by the chain of continuous practice—as no better than *aḥād*.

As a matter of fact, this is the egregious mistake that has drawn the followers of nature in this age far away from Islam. They imagine that all Islamic practices, ceremonies, worship, biographies, and histories—which cite *aḥādīth* as references—are established only on the basis of a few *aḥādīth*. But this is a clear error on their part. The *ta'āmul* [continuous practice] that our Holy Prophet[sas] established through his personal example had become so common among millions of people that had there been no trace or mention of the compilers of *aḥādīth,* even then no harm would have come to it.

Everyone has to admit that the Holy Teacher and Messenger, peace and blessings of Allah be upon him, had not so confined his teaching as to train only a few people in it and to leave all others unaware of it. Had that been so, Islam would have been so corrupted that it could not have been reformed through the efforts of any *muḥaddith* etc. Granted that the Imams of Hadith compiled thousands of *aḥādīth* relating to religious instruction, but the question is, what hadith is there that was not already being acted upon, and of which the world was wholly unaware, prior to their having written it down. If there is any teaching, or event, or doctrine, the foundation of which has been laid only by the Imams of Hadith on the basis of some report, and no sign of it is discoverable from continuous practice—of which millions of people are convinced—nor is it mentioned in the Holy Quran, then, without doubt, such a solitary report that became known a century or a century-and-a-half later, would be far removed from a level of certainty, and would deserve whatever condemnation might be directed at it. However, in reality, such *aḥādīth* have no great connection to the religion or history of Islam. If you study carefully, you will find that the Imams of Hadith have very seldom mentioned those *aḥādīth* for which no trace or mention is found in continuous practice. It is, therefore, absolutely wrong, as some ignorant ones imagine, that the world has learnt of hundreds of matters relating to the religion, even fasting and prayer services, only from the *aḥādīth* compiled by Imam Bukhārī and Muslim and others. Were the Muslims without faith for a century or a century-and-a-half? Did they not offer the daily Prayers? Did they not pay zakat? Did they not perform the hajj? Were they unaware of all the matters pertaining to Islamic doctrines mentioned in the *aḥādīth?* Certainly not! Never!

The ignorance of any person who entertains such a thought is beyond belief. Islam was as verdant and thriving before the era of the Imams of Hadith—namely Bukhārī, Muslim, etc.—as it was after their compilations; therefore, how unreasonable and unfair is it to believe dogmatically that Islam flourished only on the basis of what is known today as *aḥādīth,* which were compiled in the second century. It is a pity that not only opponents but also ignorant Muslims labour under the misconception that the Muslims were made to believe in many matters pertaining to Islam after a long time through the reports of *aḥādīth;* and that they were utterly unaware about them before those compilations.

On the contrary, the plain truth is that if the Imams of Hadith have done any favour to the people, it is only that they researched and investigated the chain of narrators to confirm the continuous practice that a world of people accepted since the beginning. They demonstrated that the beliefs and practices of the Muslims of their time were not innovations that were later intermixed with Islamic teachings; rather, they were the same practice and verbal teaching that the Holy Prophet[sas] imparted to his Companions, may Allah be pleased with them.

It is a pity that, by misconstruing this correct and factual matter, short-sighted people fell prey to an egregious error, due to which they have intensely looked down upon *aḥādīth* to this day. True, those *aḥādīth* that are outside the chain of oral tradition or practices, or which the Holy Quran does not verify, cannot be considered completely authentic. But how can the authenticity of those *aḥādīth* that have always been sustained and preserved in the continuous practice of millions of people from the very beginning, be held in suspicion and doubt? The authenticity of such *aḥādīth* cannot be doubted at all, for the overwhelming majority put them into practice and were known from generation to generation and were clearly traceable to their original source. In fact, one cannot help but consider this continued practice to be amongst the most established truths. Moreover, the Imams of Hadith buttressed this continued practice by establishing another practice, whereby they traced the chain of truthful and righteous narrators right up to the Holy Prophet, peace and blessings of Allah be upon him. So, to criticize it now is the work of only those who totally lack the insight of faith and human rationality.

After this preamble, let it also be clear that the prophecy regarding the advent of **the Promised Messiah** is not such as was recorded by the Imams of Hadith on the basis of only a few *riwāyāt* [reports]. Rather, it has been established that the Muslims adopted this prophecy as part and parcel of their faith since the early days. In other words, there were as many testimonies to the validity of this prophecy as were the number of Muslims at that time, as right from the beginning they regarded the prophecy as part of their faith.

If the **Imams of Hadith,** such as Imam Bukhārī and others, discovered anything about this prophecy by their own effort, it is only that—when they found this prophecy widespread and oft-mentioned among millions of Muslims—they, according to their practice, searched for and provided the traditional *isnād* [chains of narrators] of this well-established saying and supported it with *riwāyāt* [reports] that were *ṣaḥīḥ, marfū',* and *muttaṣil,* and which are found abundantly in their books. Besides, there seems to be no plausible reason for why, if—God forbid—it were a fabrication, the Muslims had any need for it, why they came to a consensus about it, and what compelled them to fabricate all this? On the other hand, we also see that there are many such *aḥādīth* as contain the prophecy that in the Latter Days, the ulema of this ummah will resemble the Jews, and become devoid of integrity, fear of God, and inner purity, and at that time the religion of the cross will have gained ascendancy in the world and the authority and rule of the Christian religion will have spread nearly all over the world. The fact that all these prophecies have undoubtedly been fulfilled in this age proves the authenticity of these *aḥādīth* even more clearly. Indeed, in this age, these 'ulema' of ours have become like the Jews and the dominion and the rule of the Christians has spread in the world today in a manner without any precedent in history. Since one part of this prophecy has been fulfilled so clearly and manifestly, why should the authenticity of the other part be called into question. Every sane person agrees that even if a hadith is *aḥad* and has not been widely acknowledged but contains a prophecy that is fully or partly fulfilled at its appointed time, there remains no doubt about the authenticity of such a hadith. For example, the hadith recorded in *Ṣaḥīḥ al-Bukhārī* and *Ṣaḥīḥ al-Muslim* that a fire will break out in the **Hejaz** is undoubtedly among the *aḥād.* But after the passing of nearly 600 years, this prophecy was fulfilled clearly, and even the British admit it. This prophecy was fulfilled hundreds of years after the compilation and publication of the books in which it was recorded. Can we now declare such *aḥādīth* to be absolutely unacceptable on account of their being *aḥād?* It is extremely vile and abhorrent ignorance to entertain such a thought after the authenticity of such *aḥādīth* has been established so clearly.

Think about the **prophecy** regarding the Promised Messiah in the same way. Its wording states—at places explicitly, and at other places implicitly—that the Promised Messiah will appear at a time when the rule and power of the Christians will have spread over the entire world and railway trains will be running. Moreover, most of the land will have come under cultivation, people will take keen interest in agriculture so much so that the oxen would become expensive, and there will be an abundance of canals in the world, and in terms of worldly life, it will be the time of peace.

We now find that this prophecy has been fulfilled in our time, for the Christian empire has reached such a height as if all other regimes and states are non-existent before it, and we have witnessed with our own eyes the emergence of trains, canals and widespread agriculture.

Think about it! Does not this prophecy contain such news regarding the unseen as transcends human power? Could anyone imagine the present decadent state of Islam at a time when the Islamic sword was striking the disbelievers like lightening? Can any human being possess such knowledge of the unseen as would predict a new form of transport which was previously non-existent? Look around and reflect! Is this **prophecy** not one of those grand prophecies whose reality and fulfilment could be encompassed only by the knowledge of God Almighty, and which cannot be suspected to be the work of human artifice and poor designs of the creatures?

Let it be clear that there is a whole series of such prophecies as are characterized by perfect order and exceptional eloquence and contain subtle and fine points, and matters related to the unseen and whose magnificence cannot be equalled by any human being at all. For instance, first, there are prophecies about the time of Islam's progress in connection with which it was foretold that **Chosroes** will perish and there will be no Chosroes after him; and that **Caesar** will perish and there will be no Caesar after him. And **Islam** would thrive, flourish, and spread to every nation.

It was further prophesied that in the Latter Days, most of the ulema of this ummah would resemble the **Jews** and become devoid of integrity and righteousness. **False** fatwas [edicts], evil designs, and machinations would be their religion, and they would be entrapped in **worldly** greed; and they would create a strong resemblance with the Jews, to the extent that even if a Jew had fornicated with his mother, they would also follow suit. And in that age, Christian nations would spread throughout the world and subjugate other peoples, and the love for faith would cool down in the hearts. And the religion of Islam would be afflicted by continuous and endless perils due to the spread of poisonous winds. Thereupon hardships will arise, and calamities will increase, and righteousness will continue to decrease in the hearts of Muslims, and it would be better for a person to live alone and be content with the milk of goats rather than to have anything to do with a community of Muslims. He added that when you see such conditions come to pass, you must break away from all these sects and survive on the roots of a tree until you die.

And then, in this connection, he foretold of the advent of the Promised Messiah and said that the Christian faith will be demolished at his hands, and said that he would break their cross. He did not say that he would destroy their sovereignty. This is an indication of the fact that the Promised Messiah's kingdom will be spiritual and will have nothing to do with worldly governments. On the contrary, he will fight with the strength of his blessings and will come forward into the field with the weapons of his miracles, to the extent that he will break the lustre and grandeur of the cross, and will expose the veil of the cursed and unholy doctrines of Christianity. This will be so because his light will shine like a sword and fall upon the darkness of disbelief like lightning, so much so that the seekers of truth will realize that the Living God stands with Islam.

All these prophecies—flowing like a river—are found in the *aḥādīth*. And they are so interconnected that the rejection of one necessitates the rejection of the other, and likewise, belief in one necessitates belief in the other. Who can then doubt such widespread, consistent, authentic, and coherent prophecies except the one who has crossed all limits of madness?

Can any intelligent person consider even for a second that thousands of these prophecies consisting of such extraordinary matters are mere human fabrications? The truth is that well-established, systematic, and crucial facts simply cannot be denied, because their denial necessarily leads to a great disruption and the changing of an entire world.

Besides, these prophecies contain within them a magnificent Sign of their own truth in that whatsoever was recorded in them concerning worldly revolutions—all these things appearing to be impossible—has been fulfilled. Because right from the beginning of the 13th century, internal and external crises started to exacerbate so much so that by the end of that century, the Islamic grandeur and governance had, as it were, virtually come to an end. And such catastrophes struck the Muslims in their religion and worldly affairs as if their entire world had changed. In view of these calamities, when we look upon those prophecies—which Imam Bukhārī and Imam Muslim had recorded nearly 1,100 years ago, at a time when the glory of Islam was at its zenith and the beauty of its internal state rivalled that of Yūsuf [Joseph] and the splendour of its external state put Iskandar Rūmī [Alexander the Great] to shame—our passion for faith is excited and we cannot help crying as we recall the perfect and holy revelation of our Noble Prophet[ṣas], as well as his majesty, glory, and holy influence.

Holy is Allah! What a luminous light he was, upon whom it was disclosed 1,300 years ago, how, in the beginning, his ummah will thrive, and how in an extraordinary manner it will prosper, and how in the Latter Days it will suddenly decline, and then how the Christian people will dominate the entire world in a few centuries. Remember that the Holy Prophet, peace and blessings of Allah be upon him, made a prophecy—which is recorded in *Ṣaḥīḥ al-Muslim*—concerning these times, with respect to the Promised

Messiah. He said, لَيُتْرَكَنَّ الْقِلَاصُ فَلَا يُسْعٰى عَلَيْهَا[2,1], meaning that, in the era of the Promised Messiah, the riding of camels will be abandoned. Hence, no one will mount them and make them run. This alluded to the train, after the invention of which there would be no need for making the camels run. And the camel is mentioned because it was the principal means of transport in the Arab world, onto which they could load all their household items and ride, too. This [hadith] also applies to smaller [means of transport], which are automatically included in the larger one. In short, it signifies that at that time, certain means of transport shall appear that will supersede the camel. As you now see, with the invention of the railway train, they are now doing nearly everything that the camels performed previously. Hence, which prophecy could be more evident and obvious than this one? Moreover, the Holy Quran has also foretold about this age, as it says:

وَإِذَا الْعِشَارُ عُطِّلَتْ[3]

Meaning that the Latter Days are those when the she-camel will be abandoned.

This, too, is a clear reference to the railway train. Both the afore-mentioned hadith and this verse give the same news. Since

---

1. The present day edition of *Musnad Aḥmad bin Ḥanbal* has the same wording, whereas in *Ṣaḥīḥ Muslim,* instead of وَلَيُتْرَكَنَّ the word وَلَتُتْرَكَنَّ is recorded. [Publisher]

2. *Ṣaḥīḥ al-Muslim,* Kitābul-Īmān, Ch. 71, Bābu Nuzūli-'Īsā bin Maryam [Publisher]

3. *Sūrah at-Takwīr,* 81:5 [Publisher]

there is an obvious reference to the Promised Messiah in this hadith, we must infer from it that this verse, too, speaks of the age of the Promised Messiah and implicitly refers to him. In spite of these clear testimonies that are shining bright like the sun, people still doubt these prophecies! **Let fair-minded people** decide for themselves if it is not stupidity to doubt such prophecies whose news of the unseen has visibly come true.

I am certain that what I have written so far in light of the *aḥādīth* regarding the prophecy about the Promised Messiah will suffice to satisfy a person who does not wish to unjustly oppose the truth after having found it. I have not quoted here the exact words of the *aḥādīth,* nor have I summarized all of them, because these *aḥādīth* are so well known and widespread that even young village students are familiar with them. Had I recorded in this brief booklet all the *aḥādīth* that have been narrated about this matter, I may not have completed it even after having written 10 *juzw'*.[1] But I appeal to the readers that they should carefully study *Ṣiḥāḥ Sittah* [the Six Authentic Books of Hadith] in the original or their translations, so that they might know the abundance and emphasis with which such *aḥādīth* are to be found.

THE SECOND POINT AT ISSUE was whether or not there is any mention concerning **the Promised Messiah** in the Noble Quran. Conclusive arguments render their verdict that such mention is most certainly present in the Quran. Undoubtedly, any person who ponders the following prophesies of the Noble Quran, which relate to the Latter Days of this ummat and are in this Holy

1. A *juzw'* comprises sixteen pages. [Publisher]

Book—provided that he possesses understanding and a living heart in his chest—he will have no choice but to admit that the Noble Quran categorically and definitively contains news of such a Reformer whose name, in other words, must be the Promised Messiah, not something else.

In order to understand this tiding, the following verses should first be viewed as a whole. For example, these verses:

وَالَّتِيْٓ اَحْصَنَتْ فَرْجَهَا فَنَفَخْنَا فِيْهَا مِنْ رُّوْحِنَا وَجَعَلْنٰهَا وَابْنَهَآ اٰيَةً لِّلْعٰلَمِيْنَ ○ اِنَّ هٰذِهٖٓ
اُمَّتُكُمْ اُمَّةً وَّاحِدَةً وَّاَنَا رَبُّكُمْ فَاعْبُدُوْنِ ○ وَتَقَطَّعُوْٓا اَمْرَهُمْ بَيْنَهُمْ كُلٌّ اِلَيْنَا رٰجِعُوْنَ ○ [1]
حَتّٰٓى اِذَا فُتِحَتْ يَاْجُوْجُ وَمَاْجُوْجُ وَهُمْ مِّنْ كُلِّ حَدَبٍ يَّنْسِلُوْنَ ○ وَاقْتَرَبَ الْوَعْدُ الْحَقُّ فَاِذَا
هِيَ شَاخِصَةٌ اَبْصَارُ الَّذِيْنَ كَفَرُوْا يٰوَيْلَنَا قَدْ كُنَّا فِيْ غَفْلَةٍ مِّنْ هٰذَا بَلْ كُنَّا ظٰلِمِيْنَ ○ [2]

Meaning that, God Almighty guided that woman to the right path who preserved her chastity from the *non-maḥram.* So, God breathed into her of His Spirit and made her and her son a Sign for the world. And God said, 'This ummah of yours is one ummah, and I am your Lord, so worship Me alone. But they split into many sects and divided up their ideologies, and became opposed among themselves; and in the end they will all return to Us.'[3☆] And all these sects will remain in this state until Gog and Magog are let loose and they shall hasten forth from every height and when you see that Gog and Magog have become dominant in

1. *Sūrah al-Anbiyā',* 21:92–94 [Publisher]
2. *Sūrah al-Anbiyā',* 21:97–98 [Publisher]
3. ☆ **Note:** Ezekiel, Chapter 38 and Chapter 39 verses 5–6; *Rauḍatuṣ-Ṣafā* Chapters 4, 5, and 6; and *Tafsīr Ma'ālim.* (Author)

the land, then understand that the promise of the spread of true religion has drawn nigh and that promise is:

هُوَ الَّذِيْٓ اَرْسَلَ رَسُوْلَهٗ بِالْهُدٰى وَدِيْنِ الْحَقِّ لِيُظْهِرَهٗ عَلَى الدِّيْنِ كُلِّهٖ وَلَوْ كَرِهَ الْمُشْرِكُوْنَ [1]

He further says that at the time of the manifestation of that promise, the eyes of disbelievers will stare fixedly and they will say, 'Alas for us! We were indeed heedless of this; rather, we were wrongdoers!' In other words, the truth will become manifest in an extraordinary manner and the disbelievers will realize that they were in the wrong.

The purport of all these verses is that in the Latter Days many religions will spread in the world and there will be many sects. At that time, two Christian nations will emerge and gain every single type of height. When you see that the Christian religion and Christian empires have spread in the world, you should know that the time of the fulfilment of this promise is close at hand.

At another place the Holy Quran says:

فَاِذَا جَآءَ وَعْدُ رَبِّيْ جَعَلَهٗ دَكَّآءَ وَكَانَ وَعْدُ رَبِّيْ حَقًّا ۝ وَتَرَكْنَا بَعْضَهُمْ يَوْمَئِذٍ يَّمُوْجُ فِيْ بَعْضٍ وَّنُفِخَ فِي الصُّوْرِ فَجَمَعْنٰهُمْ جَمْعًا ۝ —(Part Number 16)[2]

Meaning that, when the promise of God Almighty draws near,

1. He it is who has sent His Messenger with the guidance and the Religion of truth, that He may cause it to prevail over all religions, even if those who associate partners *with God* hate *it* (*Sūrah aṣ-Ṣaff,* 61:10). [Publisher]

2. *Sūrah al-Kahf,* 18:99–100 [Publisher]

then God Almighty will pulverize the wall, which is a defence against Gog and Magog. Indeed, the promise of God Almighty is true. And on that day—that is, during the era of the empire of Gog and Magog—We shall give respite to various sects to surge against one another. That is to say, every single sect will desire to make their religion and faith dominant over others. And just as a wave suppresses everything onto which it falls, so shall some of them fall on others to subdue them. None of them will spare any effort. Every single sect will endeavour to make their religion superior. And while they are engaged in these conflicts, God Almighty shall blow the trumpet. Then shall We gather all sects upon one religion.[1☆] The blowing of a trumpet here implies that in accordance with the practice of Allah, a reformer shall be raised by God Almighty with heavenly succour, and the spirit of life shall be breathed into his heart. And that life will be infused into others. Bear in mind that the word 'trumpet' always signifies grand revolutions. In other words, when God Almighty transforms His creatures from one state into another, the time of that transformation

1. ☆ **Footnote:** Lest some ill-informed people think that since there is a mention of Hell after both these accounts in these verses, the whole episode refers to the Hereafter as the context apparently requires. Remember, however, that it is common Quranic style, supported by hundreds of instances, that a narrative about this world is interspersed with the mention of the Hereafter. Yet, each part of the narrative has its own hallmarks that distinguish it from the other. And this pattern is abundantly found in the Holy Quran. For example, consider the miracle of *Shaqqul-Qamar,* recorded in the Holy Quran, which was a Sign. But it is immediately followed by the mention of the Hereafter, which has led some ignorant people to disregard the context and assert that the incident of *Shaqqul-Qamar* did not take place, rather it would happen on the Day of Judgement. [Author]

is described as ***nafkh-e-ṣūr*** [blowing of the trumpet]. And those blessed with visions also experience a physical manifestation of the 'trumpet' in their visions. These wonders belong to a realm whose secrets cannot be revealed to anyone in this world—except to those who have withdrawn themselves towards God.

In short, the aforementioned verses establish clearly that in the Latter Days, the Christian religion and empire will be dominant in the world and many religious disputes will arise among various nations and each nation will want to suppress the other. At such a time, the trumpet will be blown and all peoples will be gathered under the banner of Islam. That is to say, in keeping with divine practice, a heavenly dispensation shall be established with the advent of a divine **reformer.**

In fact, that very reformer is named the **Promised Messiah.** Since Christians are the source of the mischief and the main purpose of God Almighty was to destroy the glory of their cross, therefore, the person who was to be sent to invite the Christians was named Masih and **'Īsā,** in view of the condition of the addressees. The second wisdom in this [to call him the Messiah] is that when the Christians deified Ḥaḍrat 'Īsā, attributed fabrications of their own to him, hatched thousands of machinations, and exaggerated the status of Ḥaḍrat Masīḥ out of all proportion, the honour of that Living, One, and Unique God required that one of His servants from this very ummah be sent, in the name of Jesus, son of Mary, to show the miracle of His might so that it is established that to deify humans is sheer stupidity. He chooses whomsoever He pleases and can elevate the lowliest to the heavens. It should also be remembered here that when a reformer appears at a time of decadence, there is a diffusion of light from heaven. In other words, with his advent, a light also descends upon the earth and upon eager hearts. It is at this time that people spontaneously turn to the ways of goodness and virtue according to their capabilities. And every heart applies itself to deliberation and contemplation, and due to unknown reasons every eager disposition is inspired to move to seek the truth. Thereby, there blows such a breeze as inclines the eager hearts towards the Hereafter and awakens dormant faculties and it seems as if a grand revolution is about to take place.

When these signs are manifested, they testify that the reformer has come into the world. And these heavenly inspirations quicken the eager hearts in proportion to the lofty stature of the reformer. Every good-natured person awakens, though they do not know what awakens them. Every righteous person feels a change in themself, but cannot understand what has brought it about. In short, the hearts begin to stir, making the ignorant think that the awakening started by itself. But, in fact, these lights descend with the advent of a Prophet or a *Mujaddid* [Reformer]. The Holy Quran and *aḥādīth* clearly establish this fact. Allah, the Lord of Glory, says:

إِنَّآ أَنزَلْنَٰهُ فِى لَيْلَةِ ٱلْقَدْرِ ○ وَمَآ أَدْرَىٰكَ مَا لَيْلَةُ ٱلْقَدْرِ ○ لَيْلَةُ ٱلْقَدْرِ خَيْرٌ مِّنْ أَلْفِ شَهْرٍ ○
تَنَزَّلُ ٱلْمَلَٰٓئِكَةُ وَٱلرُّوحُ فِيهَا بِإِذْنِ رَبِّهِم مِّن كُلِّ أَمْرٍ ○ سَلَٰمٌ هِىَ حَتَّىٰ مَطْلَعِ ٱلْفَجْرِ ○ [1]

Meaning that, We have revealed this Book and Prophet in the Night of Destiny. And what should make you know what the Night of Destiny is? The Night of Destiny is better than a

1. *Sūrah al-Qadr,* 97:2–6 [Publisher]

thousand months. Therein descend angels and the Holy Spirit, by the command of their Lord. It is the time of peace with regard to every matter till the rising of the dawn.

Whereas, according to the prevailing doctrine of Muslims, the Night of Destiny is the name of a blessed night, yet that reality which God Almighty has revealed to me is that, in addition to the conventional meaning, the Night of Destiny is also the age when darkness spreads all over the world and there is darkness upon darkness everywhere. And that darkness itself requires that a light should descend from heaven. At that time, God Almighty causes His light-bearing angels and the Holy Spirit to descend to the earth in a manner that is consistent with their grandeur. The Holy Spirit then establishes a relationship with that *Mujaddid* and Reformer who, having been chosen and purified by God, is commissioned to invite people to the truth. The angels, too, grasp a relationship with all pious, righteous, and eager people and draw them towards virtue and place righteous abilities before them. Then peace and blessings spread in the world, and so it continues until faith reaches the perfection destined for it.

It is noteworthy that God says clearly and categorically in this blessed *sūrah* that when a reformer comes from God, the angels that are responsible for awakening the hearts do certainly descend on the earth. As a consequence of their descent, an awakening and movement towards piety and the seeking of the right path takes place in the hearts.

To think that this awakening and stirring happens by itself, without the advent of a reformer, goes against the holy Word of God Almighty and His eternal law of nature. Such objections issue from the mouths of only those who are utterly ignorant of divine secrets and who follow only their own unfounded conjectures. Rather, these are distinctive signs of the advent of the heavenly reformer and are like particles revolving around that sun. True, it is not for everyone to discover this truth. A worldly person with his obscure spiritual vision cannot discover this light; he deems religious verities and divine truths to be a laughable topic and divine insights appear to him as follies.

The following are other verses wherein the signs of the Latter Days are told. That is, firstly, they foretell that intense worldly darkness will spread all around, and then they foretell the signs of the descent of heavenly light:

إِذَا زُلْزِلَتِ الْأَرْضُ زِلْزَالَهَا ○ وَأَخْرَجَتِ الْأَرْضُ أَثْقَالَهَا ○ وَقَالَ الْإِنْسَانُ مَا لَهَا ○ يَوْمَئِذٍ
تُحَدِّثُ أَخْبَارَهَا ○ بِأَنَّ رَبَّكَ أَوْحَىٰ لَهَا ○[1]

Meaning that the Latter Days shall come at a time when the earth, in a way proportionate to its size, is violently shaken. That is to say, the inhabitants of the earth will experience a major revolution and they will incline towards selfishness and worldly pursuits. And then it is said that the earth will throw up its burdens; that is, the worldly sciences, worldly schemes, worldly cleverness, and worldly excellences, with which human nature is endowed, will altogether become manifest. Moreover, the earth on which people live will bring forth all its qualities, and many of its characteristics will be known through natural sciences and agriculture. Mines shall be dug, and land will be made fertile, causing agriculture to thrive. Also, machines of diverse types will be invented so

1. *Sūrah az-Zilzāl,* 99:2–6 [Publisher]

much so that man shall exclaim: What is this happening and how do these new and modern sciences, new arts, and new industries keep coming into being? Then will the earth, that is, the hearts of the people, effectively realize that 'we do not bring about these innovations that are currently taking place;' rather, they are the work of some kind of divine inspiration, because it is impossible for man, through his own effort, to invent such wonderful sciences in abundance.

Bear in mind that certain other verses of the Holy Quran, relating to the Hereafter, which have been included along with these verses, are actually in keeping with the same divine practice which has been mentioned earlier. But there is no doubt that the true and primary meaning of the verses is the one I have just presented. And a very cogent and decisive argument vindicates this; as the verses, if taken literally, would necessarily entail great disorder. That is to say, it is quite impossible and out of the question to interpret the verses to mean that at some point in time such devastating earthquakes would strike as would turn the earth upside down, and that, in spite of these earthquakes, people would continue to inhabit the earth. The afore-mentioned verse states clearly that men will ask, 'What is the matter with the earth?' Now, if it were really true that the earth would be turned upside down by extremely severe earthquakes, where would man be to question the earth? He would have already been buried into nothingness with the first quake.

Empirical sciences can in no way be disregarded. Therefore, to interpret the Holy Quran to mean something which is demonstrably false and inconsistent with available evidence will only lead to Islam being held up to ridicule and will afford the opponents an opportunity to raise objections against it. Therefore, the true and correct meaning of this verse is the one I have just presented. It is obviously the Christians who have brought about these unprecedented revolutions, mischiefs, and upheavals in our age which the world had never seen. This constitutes another argument to prove that the Christians are the last people who were destined to spread various mischiefs, and indeed they have worked diverse wonders in the world.

It was written that the Antichrist would claim both Prophethood and Godhead, and so it came to pass through this people. Brazen and unwarranted interpolation into the books of the Prophets on the part of the Christian clerics is, in other words, tantamount to claiming Prophethood. They have so boldly interpolated into them as if they themselves were the Prophets. They have twisted the words of the revealed books and written their commentaries to suit their purpose. Moreover, they have audaciously fabricated lies at every occasion, hiding what is present and displaying what is not present. They have so authoritatively altered the meaning of their religious books as if they received revelation and were Prophets themselves.

Therefore, it has always been observed that they intentionally opt for frivolous and false answers during debates and discussions, as if they were inventing a new Gospel of their own. In the same way, their books, too, point towards some new 'Īsā and new Gospel. They are not at all fearful when telling a lie. They have cunningly written millions of books in support of their false claim, giving the impression that they have seen Ḥaḍrat 'Īsā seated on the throne of Godhead.

As for their claim to Godhead, they have interfered excessively in the works of God. They desire not to leave any secret of the earth and heaven undiscovered. Rather, they intend to take all of God Almighty's works into their clenched fist, as well as His Godhead to the extent that, if possible, they want the rising and setting of the Sun under their own control; and for the rain to fall or not to fall subject to their will, and for nothing to remain impossible for them. What else constitutes a claim to being God? Indeed it is this, that it consists of interfering in the works and providence of God and the longing to somehow take His place.

Those who raise objections about *aḥādīth* related to the Promised Messiah and *dajjāl* must also ponder at this point that if these prophecies were not from God Almighty and were manufactured by some mere mortal, it would have been impossible for them to be fulfilled so clearly and perfectly. Was it even in anyone's fancy that in order to deify a man, the Christians would one day make such efforts and intrigues that in their philosophical writings, Divinity would no longer remain an exclusive station for God?

Look at how the distance between the ears of *dajjāl's* donkey was described to be seventy باع [*bā'*][1] which is exactly how long most railway trains are. Then, as is recorded in the Quran and *aḥādīth* that camels would no longer be used for riding, so do we witness that the railways have superseded all these forms of transportation, and camels are used infrequently. Perhaps after sometime, even this need will not remain. Similarly, we are eye-witnesses that the scholars and philosophers of this nation

1. باع [*bā'*] is a measure of distance equal to both arms spread out [Publisher].

have created such conflict in the matters of religion, the equal of which cannot to be found since Ḥaḍrat Ādam. Thus there is no doubt that they have intruded not only upon Prophethood but also upon the Divinity.

What can be a greater proof of the reliability of these *aḥādīth* than that their prophecies have been fulfilled. Moreover, the Noble Quran clearly points to this time of *dajjāl* [Antichrist] in these verses:

إِذَا زُلْزِلَتِ الْأَرْضُ زِلْزَالَهَا[1]

Anyone with the least bit of common sense can understand it. This verse indicates clearly the extent to which these people will make progress in physical sciences.

Then, as a description of this age, when new arts and sciences will be developed in the world, certain inventions and machines have been described as illustrations. They are as follows.

وَإِذَا الْأَرْضُ مُدَّتْ ○ وَأَلْقَتْ مَا فِيهَا وَتَخَلَّتْ[2]

Meaning that, when the earth would be spread—that is to say, it would be cleared—and population would swell. And whatever lies in the earth, the earth will expel it out and will become empty. That is, all its qualities will become manifest, as has been explained above.

1. When the earth is shaken with her *violent* shaking (*Sūrah az-Zilzāl,* 99:2). [Publisher]

2. *Sūrah al-Inshiqāq,* 84:4–5 [Publisher]

وَاِذَاالْعِشَارُ عُطِّلَتْ[1]

That is, when the she-camel will become useless and will not be possess any significant value. The word عِشَار [*'Ishār*] means a pregnant she-camel, which is highly prized among Arabs, and it is quite clear that this verse has nothing to do about the Day of Judgement. Judgement Day is not an occasion when a male camel will mate with a she-camel and result in a pregnancy. On the contrary, it points to the invention of railways. By using the word 'pregnant', a condition was set so that the context of this happening in this world should become clear and no doubt be left regarding its occurrence in the Hereafter.

وَاِذَاالصُّحُفُ نُشِرَتْ[2]

And when the books are disseminated and spread about. That is, the means for publishing books will become available. This refers to the abundance of printing presses and post offices in the Latter Days.

وَاِذَاالنُّفُوْسُ زُوِّجَتْ[3]

And when people are brought together. This refers to the relations between various nations and countries. It means that owing to the opening up of new routes, the availability of mailing services

1. *Sūrah at-Takwīr,* 81:5 [Publisher]
2. *Sūrah at-Takwīr,* 81:11 [Publisher]
3. *Sūrah at-Takwīr,* 81:8 [Publisher]

and the telegraph, mutual communication between people will increase. One nation will meet another and build far-reaching relationships and trade alliances, and friendly relationships between distant countries will be fostered.

وَ اِذَا الْوُحُوْشُ حُشِرَتْ[1]

And when savages will be brought together with people. That is to say, savage nations will turn towards the civilized world and will develop humane values and decency. The lowly classes will be dignified with worldly ranks and prestige, and with the spread of material sciences and arts, there will remain no distinction between the nobles and the common people. Rather, the commoners will prevail and they will hold the keys to wealth; and control of the governments will be in their hands. The substance of this verse is similar to a hadith, too.

وَ اِذَا الْبِحَارُ فُجِّرَتْ[2]

And when the rivers will be split. Meaning that, canals will sprawl the land and agriculture will boom.

وَ اِذَا الْجِبَالُ نُسِفَتْ[3]

And when the mountains will be blown away, and in them tracks

1. *Sūrah at-Takwīr,* 81:6 [Publisher]
2. *Sūrah al-Infiṭār,* 82:4 [Publisher]
3. *Sūrah al-Mursalāt,* 77:11 [Publisher]

will be built for people travelling on foot or as passengers, or for trains to move about.

In addition, signs of general darkness were described and it was said:

اِذَاالشَّمۡسُ كُوِّرَتۡ[1]

When the Sun is wrapped up. Meaning that, the world will be engulfed in extreme darkness, ignorance, and sinfulness.

وَاِذَاالنُّجُوۡمُ انۡكَدَرَتۡ[2]

And when the stars will be obscured; meaning that, when religious scholars will lose the light of sincerity.

وَاِذَاالۡكَوَاكِبُ انۡتَثَرَتۡ[3]

And when the stars will fall; meaning that, when divine scholars will pass away. For, it is impossible that people should continue to inhabit the earth while stars fall. Remember that the Gospel, too, contains a similar prophecy that the Promised Messiah will descend at a time when stars will have fallen, and the Sun and the Moon will lose their light. To take these prophecies literally is against reason. No wise person would ever suggest that when the sun literally loses its light and the stars fall to the earth—and yet the earth is

1. *Sūrah at-Takwīr,* 81:2 [Publisher]
2. *Sūrah at-Takwīr,* 81:3 [Publisher]
3. *Sūrah al-Infiṭār,* 82:3 [Publisher]

still populated with people as usual—that in this state of affairs, the Promised Messiah should come. Then it was said:

إِذَا السَّمَآءُ انْشَقَّتْ[1]

When the heavens will be torn part. Similarly, also stated:

إِذَا السَّمَآءُ انْفَطَرَتْ[2]

The Gospels, too, in the same way foretold the advent of the Promised Messiah. But these verses do not mean that the heavens will be literally torn apart and its capacities will weaken. On the contrary, what is meant is that just as something torn becomes useless, so will the heavens become unproductive. Divine grace will no longer descend from the heavens and the world will be filled with darkness and ignorance. Then, at another place it was said:

وَإِذَا الرُّسُلُ أُقِّتَتْ[3]

And when the Messengers will be brought at the appointed time. This, in fact, is an indication of the advent of the Promised Messiah and the purpose is to state that he shall descend at the precise time of need. It must be remembered that in the Word of God, the term *Rusul* [Messengers] is also used for a single [Messenger] as

1. *Sūrah al-Inshiqāq,* 84:2 [Publisher]
2. When the heaven is cleft asunder (*Sūrah al-Infiṭār,* 82:2). [Publisher]
3. *Sūrah al-Mursalāt,* 77:12 [Publisher]

well as for non-Messengers. I have explained repeatedly that many of the Quranic verses encompass multiple meanings. It is established from the *aḥādīth* that the Holy Quran has both apparent and hidden meanings. Therefore, if Messengers are to gather on the Day of Judgement as witnesses, we accept and testify to that meaning. But at this place, after describing the woeful signs of the Latter Days, when it is added at the end that the Messengers will be brought at the appointed time, the context is indicating that after darkness reaches its height, God will send a Messenger of His so that judgement may be rendered for various nations.

Since it is established from the Holy Quran that darkness will issue forth from the Christians, the chosen one of God would come to preach to them and for their judgement. Therefore, it is for this connection that he has been named ʻĪsā, because he would be sent for the Christians just as ʻĪsā, peace be on him, was sent for them. And *alif lām* [the definite article] in the verse points to a promise already made at another place, وَإِذَا الرُّسُلُ أُقِّتَتْ[1]. Meaning that, the reformer whose advent was promised by the Noble Messenger[sas] himself will be sent during the period of Christian darkness.

The Quranic verses that we have quoted thus far establish clearly that the Holy Quran certainly contains the prophecy that, in the Latter Days, the faith of the Christians will spread far and wide in the world. And they will plan for the religion of Islam to be wiped off the face of the earth and will leave no stone unturned in promoting their own faith. Then, God Almighty will turn His attention towards helping the religion of Islam and

1. *Sūrah al-Mursalāt,* 77:12 [Publisher]

will demonstrate, in such time of conflict, how He protects His religion and His Holy Word. Then, in keeping with His will and practice, a heavenly light shall descend and every fortunate person will be drawn towards it until all who hold righteousness dear to their hearts have gathered together under the banner of one faith.

God Almighty has stated in clear words that the trumpet shall be blown at the time when the clamour of debates and controversies rises. It is then that righteous people will be gathered under the banner of one Faith. Moreover, He has also stated that the Messengers will be sent at the time of darkness. Now what more can clear up this matter than Allah, the Lord of Glory, stating that the **FIRST** sign of the Latter Days will be the dominance of Gog and Magog, i.e. the influence of Russia and the British. The **SECOND** sign will be the emergence of many sects. The **THIRD** sign is that these sects will feud with one another and would fall upon one another like waves. The **FOURTH** sign will be the development of railways. The **FIFTH** sign will be the means for publishing books and newspapers, such as the press and the telegraph. The **SIXTH** sign will be the digging of canals. The **SEVENTH** will be the increase in population and cultivation of the earth. The **EIGHTH** sign will be the blowing away of the mountains. The **NINTH** sign will be the progress of all modern sciences and arts. The **TENTH** sign will be the spread of sinfulness and darkness and the disappearance of righteousness, purity, and the light of faith from the world.

The **ELEVENTH** sign will be the emergence of *dābbatul-arḍ,* that is, a surge in preachers who would be totally devoid of heavenly light and who will be like earthly worms. Their works will side with *Dajjāl* [the Antichrist] whereas their words will side with Islam. That is, their deeds would be in service of *Dajjāl*—ugly and animal-like—yet their speech will be like that of humans. The **TWELFTH** sign will be the advent of the Promised Messiah, which is described metaphorically as *nafkh-e-ṣūr,* [blowing of the trumpet] in the Holy Quran. In reality, this *nafkh* [blowing] is of two kinds: one is the inspiration that leads one astray and the other is the inspiration that guides one aright, as is referred to in the following verse:

وَنُفِخَ فِي الصُّوْرِ فَصَعِقَ مَنْ فِي السَّمٰوٰتِ وَمَنْ فِي الْاَرْضِ اِلَّا مَنْ شَآءَ اللّٰهُ ؕ ثُمَّ نُفِخَ فِيْهِ اُخْرٰى
فَاِذَا هُمْ قِيَامٌ يَّنْظُرُوْنَ[1]

These verses have two meanings: they are related to the Day of Judgement and also to this world. They are like the verse:

اِعْلَمُوْٓا اَنَّ اللّٰهَ يُحْيِ الْاَرْضَ بَعْدَ مَوْتِهَا[2]

And the verse:

فَسَالَتْ اَوْدِيَةٌۢ بِقَدَرِهَا[3]

1. And the trumpet will be blown, and *all* who are in the heavens and *all* who are in the earth will *fall down in a* swoon, except those whom Allah will please *to exempt.* Then will it be blown a second time, and lo! they will be standing, awaiting (*Sūrah az-Zumar,* 39:69). [Publisher]

2. Know that Allah is *now* quickening the earth after its death (*Sūrah al-Ḥadīd,* 57:18). [Publisher]

3. So that valleys flow according to their measure (*Sūrah ar-Ra'd,* 13:18). [Publisher]

With regard to this world, these verses mean that the Latter Days shall consist of two periods. The first period will be of ignorance, when heedlessness will overcomes everyone earthly and heavenly—i.e. every unfortunate and fortunate one—except those whom Allah saves. Thereafter, there will come a second period, of guidance, when people will suddenly arise and begin to see. That is, their negligence will vanish and their hearts will be filled with enlightenment. The unfortunate will become aware of their misfortune even though they might not come to believe.

Apart from these, there are many other verses of the Holy Quran that speak of the Latter Days and of the advent of the Promised Messiah; but their blessed meanings are derived from profound insights. That is why a superficial-minded person cannot grasp them, nor can any naïve person comprehend these subtle points. One of those verses is the following:

إِنَّآ أَرْسَلْنَآ إِلَيْكُمْ رَسُولًا شَاهِدًا عَلَيْكُمْ كَمَآ أَرْسَلْنَآ إِلَىٰ فِرْعَوْنَ رَسُولًا[1]

It is quite clear that the word كَمَا [*kamā*—meaning 'just as'] indicates that our Holy Prophet, peace and blessings of Allah be upon him, is **the like of Moses.** In the Torah, Deuteronomy,[2] too, the Holy Prophet, peace and blessings of Allah be upon him, is described as the like of Moses. Obviously, the resemblance referred to is a perfect resemblance, not imperfect. For, were it imperfect,

1. Verily, We have sent to you a Messenger, who is a witness over you, just as We sent a Messenger to Pharaoh (*Sūrah al-Muzzammil*, 73:16). [Publisher]

2. Deuteronomy, 18:18 [Publisher]

there would remain no distinction for the Holy Prophet, peace and blessings of Allah be upon him. This is because there are many Prophets who bore some resemblance with Moses in that they, too, raised the sword by the command of God, waged wars and emerged victorious in miraculous ways. But can any of these Prophets be the object of this prophecy? Not at all! In short, the Holy Prophet, may peace be on him, can be its specific object only if the resemblance is understood to be a **perfect resemblance.** And one of the greatest elements of this perfect resemblance is that after honouring Moses[as] as His Messenger, God Almighty, out of His many blessings and favours upon him, placed in his dispensation, a long series of spiritual and worldly successors. This period lasted for nearly 1,400 years and **ended** with Ḥaḍrat ʻĪsā, peace be upon him. During this time, hundreds of kings and recipients of revelation were born in the Mosaic dispensation. And God continued to help the followers of the law of Moses in wonderful ways, the amazing accounts of which were preserved in the pages of history. As Allah, the Lord of Glory, says:

وَلَقَدْ اٰتَيْنَا مُوْسَى الْكِتٰبَ وَقَفَّيْنَا مِنْۢ بَعْدِهٖ بِالرُّسُلِ[1]

ثُمَّ قَفَّيْنَا عَلٰۤى اٰثَارِهِمْ بِرُسُلِنَا وَقَفَّيْنَا بِعِيْسَى ابْنِ مَرْيَمَ وَاٰتَيْنٰهُ الْاِنْجِيْلَ ۙ وَجَعَلْنَا فِيْ قُلُوْبِ الَّذِيْنَ اتَّبَعُوْهُ رَاْفَةً وَّرَحْمَةً[2]

Meaning that, We gave Moses a book and many Prophets came after him. After all of them, We sent Jesus, son of Mary, and We

1. *Sūrah al-Baqarah,* 2:88 [Publisher]

2. *Sūrah al-Ḥadīd,* 57:28 [Publisher]

gave him the Gospel. And We placed compassion and mercy in the hearts of those who accepted him. That is, they preached with meekness, modesty, and politeness, instead of the sword.

This verse suggests that even though the Mosaic Law was awe-inspiring, and hundreds of thousands were killed in compliance with its injunctions, even nearly 400,000 infants were also slain, God Almighty willed that this dispensation should come to end in mercy, and He may create a people from among them who would guide human beings to the right path, not with the sword, but with their knowledge, moral character, and power of purification.

Because **resemblance in blessings** is of utmost importance, and perfect resemblance can be established only if resemblance in blessings is also established; therefore, it so happened that Ḥaḍrat Mūsā, peace be on him, was blessed with servants of his law for nearly 1,400 years, among whom were Prophets and recipients of revelation, and that dispensation ended with a Prophet who called towards the truth with compassion and humility, and not with the sword. Similarly, our Holy Prophet, peace and blessings of Allah be upon him, was also blessed with the servants of Shariah who—according to the hadith, عُلَمَآءُ أُمَّتِيْ كَأَنْبِيَآءِ بَنِيْ إِسْرَآئِيْل[1]—were *Mulhamīn* and *Muḥaddathīn* [i.e. recipients of revelation and divine converse]. And just as Ḥaḍrat Masīḥ, peace be upon him, who invited towards truth with compassion and humility and not with the sword, was sent at the end of Mosaic dispensation, similarly, God sent the Promised

1. The scholars of my ummah are like the Prophets of Banī Isrā'īl. [Publisher]

Messiah for this Shariah, so that he, too, should invite towards righteousness with only compassion, mercy, and heavenly light. And just as Ḥaḍrat Masīḥ came around 1,400 years after Ḥaḍrat Mūsā [Moses], peace be upon him, so has this Promised Messiah appeared at the beginning of the 14th century after Hijra. And thus, a perfect resemblance between the Muhammadan dispensation and the Mosaic dispensation was established.

If it is said that in the Mosaic dispensation, Prophets came to promote the faith and Ḥaḍrat Masīḥ, too, was a Prophet, the answer is that both Prophet and *Muḥaddath* enjoy the same status of a *Mursal* [i.e. one who is sent by God]. Just as God has named Prophets as *Mursalīn* [the commissioned ones], so has He named *Muḥaddathīn* [recipients of divine converse] as *Mursalīn*. It is with the purpose of indicating this that the Holy Quran says:

وَقَفَّيْنَا مِنْۢ بَعْدِهٖ بِالرُّسُلِ[1]

God did not say, قَفَّيْنَا مِنْ بَعْدِهٖ بِالْأَنْبِيَاءِ ['caused after him Prophets to follow in his footsteps'], which points to the fact that رُسُل [*Rusul*] here signifies *Mursalīn,* be they Prophets, Messengers, or *Muḥaddathīn.*

Since our Noble Master and Prophet, peace and blessings of Allah be upon him, is *Khātamun-Nabiyyīn* [the Seal of the Prophets] and no Prophet can come after the Holy Prophet, peace and blessings of Allah be on him, that is why, in the Islamic dispensation, ***Muhaddathīn* have been appointed in place** of Prophets. The following verses refers precisely to this:

1. And caused after him Messengers to follow in his footsteps (*Sūrah al-Baqarah,* 2:88). [Publisher]

ثُلَّةٌ مِّنَ الْأَوَّلِيْنَ ○ وَ ثُلَّةٌ مِّنَ الْاٰخِرِيْنَ ○[1]

Since the word ثُلَّةٌ [a large party] occurs equally in both verses, it is categorically established that the *Muḥaddathīn* of this ummah are no less in terms of their number and the duration of succession than the *Mursalīn* of the Mosaic dispensation. In fact, another verse refers to this point too:

وَعَدَ اللّٰهُ الَّذِيْنَ اٰمَنُوْا مِنْكُمْ وَ عَمِلُوا الصّٰلِحٰتِ لَيَسْتَخْلِفَنَّهُمْ فِي الْاَرْضِ كَمَا اسْتَخْلَفَ الَّذِيْنَ مِنْ قَبْلِهِمْ ۪ وَ لَيُمَكِّنَنَّ لَهُمْ دِيْنَهُمُ الَّذِي ارْتَضٰى لَهُمْ وَ لَيُبَدِّلَنَّهُمْ مِّنْۢ بَعْدِ خَوْفِهِمْ اَمْنًا ؕ يَعْبُدُوْنَنِيْ لَا يُشْرِكُوْنَ بِيْ شَيْـًٔا[2]

Meaning that, God has promised those among you who believe and do good works, that He will surely make them successors in the earth, as He made successors from among those who were before them; that He will surely establish for them their religion which He has chosen for them; and that He will surely give them security and peace in exchange after their fear. They will worship Me alone, and they will not associate anything with Me. (Part Number 18, *Sūrah an-Nūr*)

Now ponder carefully over this verse. It, too, refers clearly to the above resemblance. And if the resemblance is not a perfect resemblance, then these verses become absurd, because in the Mosaic dispensation, the period of *Khilāfat* [leadership by succession] stretched for 1,400 years, and not just to 30 years. There

1. A large party from among the early ones; and a large party from among the later ones (*Sūrah al-Wāqi'ah*, 56:40–41). [Publisher]

2. *Sūrah an-Nūr*, 24:56 [Publisher]

appeared hundreds of *Khulafā',* both spiritual and worldly, not just four, and then it terminated forever.

And to say that the word مِنْکُم [*minkum*—from among you] signifies that the *Khulafā'* will be solely from among the Companions because they are the sole addressees of the word *minkum,* then such thinking would be a blatant mistake. Such words can only be uttered by a person who has never read the Holy Quran with reflection and has failed to understand its manner of expression. If it were true that the only intended addressees were those believers who were alive and present at the time [of its revelation], then such a view would render the interpretation of the entire Quran upside down.

For example, there is another Quranic verse similar to the above-mentioned verse in which, according to the literal wording, the addressees are the believers of Ḥaḍrat Mūsā who were alive in his lifetime. In fact, there are very strong indications from the context that they are in reality the addressees of the following verses:

قَالَ سَنُقَتِّلُ اَبۡنَآءَهُمۡ وَ نَسۡتَحۡیٖ نِسَآءَهُمۡ وَ اِنَّا فَوۡقَهُمۡ قٰهِرُوۡنَ ○ قَالَ مُوۡسٰی لِقَوۡمِهِ
اسۡتَعِیۡنُوۡا بِاللّٰهِ وَ اصۡبِرُوۡا اِنَّ الۡاَرۡضَ لِلّٰهِ یُوۡرِثُهَا مَنۡ یَّشَآءُ مِنۡ عِبَادِهٖ وَ الۡعَاقِبَةُ لِلۡمُتَّقِیۡنَ ○
قَالُوۡۤا اُوۡذِیۡنَا مِنۡ قَبۡلِ اَنۡ تَاۡتِیَنَا وَ مِنۡۢ بَعۡدِ مَا جِئۡتَنَا قَالَ عَسٰی رَبُّکُمۡ اَنۡ یُّهۡلِکَ عَدُوَّکُمۡ وَ
یَسۡتَخۡلِفَکُمۡ فِی الۡاَرۡضِ فَیَنۡظُرَ کَیۡفَ تَعۡمَلُوۡنَ ○—*Part Number 9, Sūrah al-A'rāf*[1]

Meaning that Pharaoh said, 'We will slay the sons of Banī Isrā'īl and let their daughters live. And surely we are dominant over them.' Then Moses said to his people, 'Seek help from Allah and

1. *Sūrah al-A'rāf,* 7:128–130 [Publisher]

be patient. Verily, the earth is Allah's; He gives it as a heritage to whomsoever He pleases of His servants, and the good end is for the righteous.' Then the people of Moses said to him, 'We were persecuted before you and even after you came to us.' He said, 'Your Lord is about to destroy your enemy and make you successors in the land, that He may then see how you act.'

Now, in these verses, those followers of Ḥaḍrat Mūsā who were alive in his time are clearly and categorically the addressed people. They were the ones who had complained of the atrocities of Pharaoh and had said 'we were persecuted before you came and then even after you had come.' And it was they who were told that they should patiently bear these hardships, God would turn towards them with His mercy and destroy their enemy, and make them *Khulafā'* in the land. But it is clear to historians, and those who study Jewish and Christian texts know very well, that although the enemy of this nation—that is, Pharaoh—perished in front of them, they themselves were not blessed with either worldly or spiritual *Khilāfat.* Rather, most of them were destroyed because of their own disobedience.

They succumbed to death after wandering in the bleak and barren wilderness for forty years. Then, after their death, there began such a long line of succession among their progeny that there arose among this nation many kings. And indeed divinely appointed *Khulafā'* such as David and Solomon were born among these very people until finally this chain of *Khulafā'* came to its culmination in the 14th century with Ḥaḍrat Masīḥ. Thus, it is clear that addressing an existing people does not at all mean that address necessarily remain confined to the people of that time. On the contrary, it is indeed the case with Quranic idiom that oftentimes it addresses one people, but its true addressees are another people who have either passed away or are yet to come. For example, in *Sūrah al-Baqarah,* Allah, the Lord of Glory, addresses the Jews who were present at that time and says:

يٰبَنِيْٓ اِسْرَآءِيْلَ اذْكُرُوْا نِعْمَتِيَ الَّتِيْٓ اَنْعَمْتُ عَلَيْكُمْ وَ اَوْفُوْا بِعَهْدِيْٓ اُوْفِ بِعَهْدِكُمْ وَ اِيَّايَ
فَارْهَبُوْنِ[1]

Meaning that, O children of Israel! Remember that favour which I bestowed upon you, and fulfil your covenant with Me, so that I too may fulfil My covenant with you, and fear Me alone.

Now it is clear that the Jews of the time of the Holy Prophet were proof of ضُرِبَتْ عَلَيْهِمُ الذِّلَّةُ [having been smitten with abasement]; they were certainly not the recipients of any favour, and nor was this pledge taken from them that they would believe in *Khātamul-Anbiyā'* [the Seal of the Prophets]. Then after this it was said:

وَ اِذْ نَجَّيْنٰكُمْ مِّنْ اٰلِ فِرْعَوْنَ يَسُوْمُوْنَكُمْ سُوْٓءَ الْعَذَابِ يُذَبِّحُوْنَ اَبْنَآءَكُمْ وَ يَسْتَحْيُوْنَ نِسَآءَكُمْ
وَ فِيْ ذٰلِكُمْ بَلَآءٌ مِّنْ رَّبِّكُمْ عَظِيْمٌ ۝ وَ اِذْ فَرَقْنَا بِكُمُ الْبَحْرَ فَاَنْجَيْنٰكُمْ وَ اَغْرَقْنَآ اٰلَ فِرْعَوْنَ وَ
اَنْتُمْ تَنْظُرُوْنَ ۝[2]

Meaning that, And remember the time when We delivered you from Pharaoh's people. They used to inflict upon you various types of suffering, slaying your sons and sparing your daughters; and in that there was a great trial for you from God Almighty.

1. *Sūrah al-Baqarah,* 2:41 [Publisher]

2. *Sūrah al-Baqarah,* 2:50–51 [Publisher]

And remember the time when We divided the sea just when you reached there, and then We saved you and drowned the people of Pharaoh, while you looked on.

Now, it should be considered that from among these incidents, not even one was faced by the Jews who were present at the time of the Holy Prophet, peace and blessings of Allah be upon him. Neither were they afflicted with suffering at the hand of the Pharaoh, nor did anyone kill their sons, nor did they have to cross any sea.

Then further ahead He says:

وَ اِذْ قُلْتُمْ يٰمُوْسٰى لَنْ نُّؤْمِنَ لَكَ حَتّٰى نَرَى اللّٰهَ جَهْرَةً فَاَخَذَتْكُمُ الصّٰعِقَةُ وَ اَنْتُمْ تَنْظُرُوْنَ ○ ثُمَّ بَعَثْنٰكُمْ مِّنْۢ بَعْدِ مَوْتِكُمْ لَعَلَّكُمْ تَشْكُرُوْنَ ○ وَ ظَلَّلْنَا عَلَيْكُمُ الْغَمَامَ وَ اَنْزَلْنَا عَلَيْكُمُ الْمَنَّ وَ السَّلْوٰى ـ [1]

Meaning that, And remember the time when you said to Moses that We will not believe merely because of what you say until we ourselves see Allah with our own eyes. Thereupon thunderbolt fell upon you; and then you were given life, that you might be grateful. And We caused the clouds to be a shade over you and sent down *mann* and *salwā* [quails] for you.

Now it is obvious that Moses[as] had died 2,000 years before the Jews who were addressed in the Holy Quran; and there was not a trace of them in the time of Moses[as]. How, then, could they have put such questions to Moses[as]? Where did the thunderbolt fall upon them and where did they eat *mann* and *salwā*? Were they present in the time of Moses[as] in some other bodily forms,

1. *Sūrah al-Baqarah,* 2:56–58 [Publisher]

and then reappeared, by way of reincarnation, in the time of the Holy Prophet, peace and blessings of Allah be upon him? And if this is not the case, then what can we say other than to make an interpretation that the people who are being addressed need not be the ones to whom the attributed incidents actually relate.

It is an established characteristic of the Holy Quran and *aḥādīth* that oftentimes some event is attributed to a person or a people, but actually that event relates to another person or another people. And under this heading is news of the coming of Jesus, son of Mary; because in some *aḥādīth,* the event of coming in the Latter Days has been attributed to Jesus while, in fact, he had already died. This incident is thus also attributed to Ḥaḍrat Masīḥ in the same way that being delivered from the Pharaoh, the eating of *mann* and *salwā,* the falling of the thunderbolt, the crossing of the sea, the episode of لَنْ نَّصْبِرَ عَلٰى طَعَامٍ وَّاحِدٍ[1] [We will not remain content with one kind of food] were ascribed to those Jews who were present in the time of the Holy Prophet, peace and blessings of Allah be upon him, whereas these incidents happened to their earlier people, who had passed away hundreds of years before them.

Thus if someone, while interpreting verses of the Holy Quran, does not ponder their rational side and deems it obligatory to adhere to the literal words, then at the very least it would be established from these verses that the doctrine of transmigration is true. Otherwise, how was it possible that God should have attributed the act of an agent to someone else who has nothing

1. *Sūrah al-Baqarah,* 2:62 [Publisher]

to do at all with the carrying out of that action, while He Himself says:

لَا تَزِرُ وَازِرَةٌ وِّزْرَ اُخْرٰى[1]

Similarly, if the people of Moses[as] had disobeyed him and were struck by the thunderbolt, or they had worshipped the calf and were smitten by chastisement, then what did this other people, who were born 2,000 years later, have to do with these incidents? Generally speaking, from the time of Ḥaḍrat Ādam[as] to this day, the earlier people are like ancestors to the later ones, but no one's sin can be attributed to someone else. In addition, there is God Almighty's saying in the Holy Quran that you disobeyed Moses[as] and you said that 'we would not believe in God until we saw Him face-to-face', and owing to this sin the thunderbolt struck you: Taken literally, how can we interpret all these statements except to say that, in fact, all the Jews who were alive in the time of the Holy Prophet, peace and blessings of Allah be upon him, were also alive in the time of Moses[as]; and on them indeed had descended *mann* and *salwā,* and the thunderbolt had in fact struck them, and they were actually the ones for whose sake the Pharaoh was killed and, moreover, the same Jews were reincarnated in the time of the Holy Prophet, peace and blessings of Allah be upon him; and therefore, addressing them as such was justified.

But the question is, why are such clear and simple meanings not accepted. Are they beyond the power of God Almighty? And

1. And no bearer of burden shall bear the burden of another (*Sūrah Banī Isrā'īl,* 17:16). [Publisher]

why instead are those meanings accepted that fall under the category of far-fetched interpretations? Is God Almighty not powerful enough to have brought the Jews of the time of Moses[as] back to life in the time of the Holy Prophet, peace and blessings of Allah be upon him, by way of reincarnation, just as our opponents believe that He will bring back Ḥaḍrat 'Īsā, in his physical body from the heaven at some point in time after hundreds of years? When it is accepted on the basis of unfounded sayings that the soul of Ḥaḍrat 'Īsā will return to the world, then why and on what basis should it not be accepted that the souls of all those Jews mentioned in the manifest and explicit Quranic text had returned to the world in the time of the Holy Prophet, peace and blessings of Allah be upon him, by way of reincarnation? Look, God Almighty clearly says:

وَ اِذْ قُلْتُمْ يٰمُوْسٰى لَنْ نُّؤْمِنَ لَكَ حَتّٰى نَرَى اللّٰهَ جَهْرَةً فَاَخَذَتْكُمُ الصّٰعِقَةُ وَ اَنْتُمْ تَنْظُرُوْنَ[1]

Meaning that, remember the time when you, and not someone else, said that we will not believe in you just because you ask us until we see God face-to-face. Then a thunderstorm struck you while you were watching.

There is another subtle point in this verse; namely, that God Almighty did not declare the Jews [in the time of the Holy Prophet[sas]] as the successors of the past generation. Rather, He addressed them as if they themselves were the Jews of old. Thus, in this case, the Holy Quran has given the Jews in the time of the Holy Prophet, peace and blessings of Allah be upon him, the

1. *Sūrah al-Baqarah,* 2:56 [Publisher]

exact same names of the earlier Banī Isrā'īl. Therefore, since these people have been declared to be those very same people, it necessitates that they also have the same names. The reason is that names are for historical facts like organs are for the body from which they cannot be separated; and essential 'organs' [i.e. names] cannot be separated from their corresponding facts.

Now consider well that, while addressing the Jews in the time of the Holy Prophet, peace and blessings of Allah be upon him, God Almighty said in clear and categorical terms that you indeed were the ones who committed such and such wicked deeds in the time of Moses[as]. Then how unjust and wrongful is it to subject such a clear and explicit verse to various interpretations; but on the basis of *aḥādīth* alone, to bring Jesus[as] back to earth even though his death is clearly established from the Holy Quran.

Dear friends! If it is indeed the way and practice of God Almighty that He brings people of the past back into the world, then the definitive text of the Holy Quran that repeatedly addresses the dead, and thus testifies to their lives, can never be legitimately ignored. But if, in this context, you fear that even though such meanings are not beyond the power of God Almighty, they nonetheless defy reason and, therefore, you incline towards such interpretations and meanings as are not contrary to reason, then the prophecy regarding the coming of Jesus must indeed be interpreted in the same way. Because if reason opposes the Jews of the past coming back to life in the blessed ministry of our Holy Prophet, peace and blessings of Allah be upon him, or if the returning of their souls by way of transmigration seems unreasonable, then why is it suggested that Ḥaḍrat Masīḥ will return to the world, despite the following verse giving a loud and clear testimony concerning his death:

فَلَمَّا تَوَفَّيْتَنِىْ كُنْتَ اَنْتَ الرَّقِيْبَ عَلَيْهِمْ [1]

Is the return of the souls of the Jews to the world irrational and beyond the powers of God Almighty, and yet the return of Ḥaḍrat 'Īsā to the earth in his physical body quite rational? Moreover, if on account of the impossibility of literal meanings, the clear and obvious statements of the Holy Quran are interpreted to mean something other than their apparent meanings, then why can we not interpret *aḥādīth* to mean something other than their apparent and literal meanings? Is the status of *aḥādīth* higher than that of the Holy Quran that we must always stick to their literal meanings, however irrational, yet subject the Holy Quran to various interpretations?

To revert to the main subject, some people deny the general application of the verse:

وَعَدَ اللّٰهُ الَّذِيْنَ اٰمَنُوْا مِنْكُمْ وَ عَمِلُوا الصّٰلِحٰتِ لَيَسْتَخْلِفَنَّهُمْ فِى الْاَرْضِ كَمَا اسْتَخْلَفَ الَّذِيْنَ مِنْ قَبْلِهِمْ [2]

They say that the word مِنْكُمْ [*minkum*—from among you] in the

1. [Jesus[as] said to God:] But since You caused me to die, You have been the Watcher over them (*Sūrah al-Mā'idah,* 5:118). [Publisher]

2. Allah has promised to those among you who believe and do good works that He will surely make them Successors in the earth, as He made Successors *from among* those who were before them (*Sūrah an-Nūr,* 24:56). [Publisher]

verse refers only to the Companions and that true *Khilāfat* ended in their age, so that henceforth there would be no trace of *Khilāfat* in Islam until the Day of Judgement; as if, like a short-lived dream, *Khilāfat* lasted for only thirty years and, thereafter, Islam suffered an eternal doom. But may I ask: Can any righteous person believe that the blessings of the shariah of Moses[as] and his *Khilāfat* continued for 1,400 years without interruption, but the blessings of that Prophet[sas] —who has been declared to be 'the Most Exalted Messenger' and 'the Best of all the Prophets' and whose shariah will last till doomsday—were limited really only to his own time and God Almighty did not desire that examples of his blessings should be manifested through his spiritual *Khulafā'* for a long time to come? I shudder at hearing such statements. It is a pity that such people, too, are indeed called Muslims who utter such blasphemous words, by way of complete insolence and cunning, that apparently the future holds no more Islamic blessings; rather, they have long since come to an end.

Besides, it is strange logic to infer from the word *minkum* that since the Companions were the prime addressees, therefore, this *Khilāfat* was limited to them. If the Holy Quran were interpreted in this way, it would amount to a bigger transgression than that of the Jews. Now let it be clear that the word *minkum* has occurred approximately eighty-two times in the Holy Quran and on all those occasions, except for two or three where a specific context has been given, the word *minkum* stands invariably for all the Muslims who will be born until doomsday.

Now, by way of example, I write a few of those verses in which the word *minkum* is found:

(1) فَمَنْ كَانَ مِنْكُمْ مَّرِيْضًا اَوْ عَلٰى سَفَرٍ فَعِدَّةٌ مِّنْ اَيَّامٍ اُخَرَ [1]

Meaning that, whoso among you is sick or is on a journey should fast the same number of other days. Now think whether this injunction was exclusively for the Companions[ra], or whether all other Muslims who will be born till doomsday are its addressees? Likewise, ponder over the following verses:

(2) ذٰلِكَ يُوْعَظُ بِهٖ مَنْ كَانَ مِنْكُمْ يُؤْمِنُ بِاللّٰهِ وَالْيَوْمِ الْاٰخِرِ [2]

Meaning that, this is an admonition for he among you who believes in Allah and the Last Day.

(3) وَالَّذِيْنَ يُتَوَفَّوْنَ مِنْكُمْ وَيَذَرُوْنَ اَزْوَاجًا [3]

Meaning that, and those of you who die and leave wives behind.

(4) وَلْتَكُنْ مِّنْكُمْ اُمَّةٌ يَّدْعُوْنَ اِلَى الْخَيْرِ وَيَاْمُرُوْنَ بِالْمَعْرُوْفِ وَيَنْهَوْنَ عَنِ الْمُنْكَرِ [4]

Meaning that, there should be among you such people who should invite to goodness, enjoin equity, and forbid evil.

(5) اَنِّيْ لَاۤ اُضِيْعُ عَمَلَ عَامِلٍ مِّنْكُمْ مِّنْ ذَكَرٍ اَوْ اُنْثٰى [5]

---

1. *Sūrah al-Baqarah,* 2:185 [Publisher]
2. *Sūrah al-Baqarah,* 2:233 [Publisher]
3. *Sūrah al-Baqarah,* 2:235 [Publisher]
4. *Sūrah Āl 'Imrān,* 3:105 [Publisher]
5. *Sūrah Āl 'Imrān,* 3:196 [Publisher]

I will allow not the work of any worker from among you, whether male or female, to be lost.

(6) لَا تَأْكُلُوٓا اَمْوَالَكُمْ بَيْنَكُمْ بِالْبَاطِلِ اِلَّآ اَنْ تَكُوْنَ تِجَارَةً عَنْ تَرَاضٍ مِّنْكُمْ[1]

Devour not your property among yourselves by unlawful means, except that you earn by trade with mutual consent.

(7) وَاِنْ كُنْتُمْ جُنُبًا فَاطَّهَّرُوْا وَاِنْ كُنْتُمْ مَّرْضٰٓى اَوْ عَلٰى سَفَرٍ اَوْ جَآءَ اَحَدٌ مِّنْكُمْ مِّنَ الْغَآئِطِ اَوْ لٰمَسْتُمُ النِّسَآءَ فَلَمْ تَجِدُوْا مَآءً فَتَيَمَّمُوْا صَعِيْدًا طَيِّبًا[2]

Meaning that, if you are ill or on a journey, or come from the privy, or you have touched women, and you find not water, then in all these circumstances, betake yourselves to pure dust.

(8) اَطِيْعُوا الرَّسُوْلَ وَاُولِي الْاَمْرِ مِنْكُمْ[3]

Meaning that, obey Allah, the Messenger, and your sovereigns.

(9) مَنْ عَمِلَ مِنْكُمْ سُوْٓءًا بِجَهَالَةٍ ثُمَّ تَابَ مِنْۢ بَعْدِهٖ وَاَصْلَحَ فَاَنَّهٗ غَفُوْرٌ رَّحِيْمٌ[4]

Meaning that, whichever person from among you commits any evil deed due to his ignorance, and then repents and becomes occupied with doing good deeds, then Allah is Most Forgiving, Merciful.

1. *Sūrah an-Nisā',* 4:30 [Publisher]
2. *Sūrah al-Mā'idah,* 5:7 [Publisher]
3. *Sūrah an-Nisā',* 4:60 [Publisher]
4. *Sūrah al-An'ām,* 6:55 [Publisher]

(10) فَمَا جَزَآءُ مَنْ يَّفْعَلُ ذٰلِكَ مِنْكُمْ اِلَّا خِزْيٌ فِي الْحَيٰوةِ الدُّنْيَا وَ يَوْمَ الْقِيٰمَةِ يُرَدُّوْنَ اِلٰٓى اَشَدِّ الْعَذَابِ[1]

Meaning that, whichever person among you commits such a deed shall face disgrace in the present life; and on the Day of Judgement, there is for him a severe punishment.

(11) وَاِنْ مِّنْكُمْ اِلَّا وَارِدُهَا[2]

Meaning that, there is not one from among you who shall not come to hell.

(12) وَلَقَدْ عَلِمْنَا الْمُسْتَقْدِمِيْنَ مِنْكُمْ وَلَقَدْ عَلِمْنَا الْمُسْتَاْخِرِيْنَ[3]

Meaning that, we do know those people from among you who will move ahead and those who will lag behind.

Reflect over all these places where the word مِنْكُمْ [*minkum*—from among you] has been used for all the Muslims, regardless of whether they were alive at that time or will be born until doomsday. Similarly, in all other instances, except for two or three places, the word has been used in a general sense. Seemingly, the Companions[ra] were indeed the direct addressees of all the injunctions, but unless there is a specific context, applying them exclusively to the Companions[ra] is not permissible. Otherwise, every sinner can argue that the Companions[ra] were the sole addressees of the injunctions regarding prayer, fasting, hajj, piety, cleanliness, and avoidance of sins, therefore, they are not

1. *Sūrah al-Baqarah,* 2:86 [Publisher]
2. *Sūrah Maryam,* 19:72 [Publisher]
3. *Sūrah al-Ḥijr,* 15:25 [Publisher]

obligated to follow the injunctions concerning prayers, fasting, etc. And clearly, only a heretic, and not any God-fearing person, can utter such words.

If someone were to think that the verse,[1] وَعَدَ اللّٰهُ الَّذِيْنَ اٰمَنُوْا, has general application—that is, its true purpose was to apply to all people and not just a specific people—then why was the word مِنْكُمْ [*minkum*—from among you] added here? And what indeed was the need for this addition? It would have be enough to say this much that: وعد الله الذين آمنوا وعملوا الصلحت ليستخلفنهم في الأرض كما استخلف الذين من قبلهم. [Allah has promised to those who believe and do good works that He will surely make them Successors in the earth, as He made Successors *from among* those who were before them]. The answer to this question is that this promise was made against the backdrop of the believers and righteous people who had passed away before this ummah. In other words, this verse explains that God Almighty, before you, made those people *Khulafā'* in the earth who were righteous and pious and whose faith was accompanied by righteous deeds. Therefore, O Muslims! God promises that from among you, too, He will make such people *Khulafā'* as would possess these same qualities and whose faith would be accompanied by righteous deeds. Hence, the word *minkum* is not added unnecessarily; rather, it is employed to refer to the righteous and pious people of Islam. The words 'believers' and 'righteous' apply equally to the believers and the righteous ones of the previous ummahs and of this ummah; thus, if there was no

---

1. Allah has promised to those who believe (*Sūrah an-Nūr,* 24:56). [Publisher]

extra word to distinguish between them, the text would be poor, ambiguous, and far removed from eloquence.

The word *minkum* also emphasizes the point that just as in the past, when only the righteous and pious were appointed *Khulafā',* so, likewise from among you, only the righteous and pious people will be appointed *Khulafā'.* Now, the discerning eye can see that in keeping with the general idiom, the word *minkum* is not unnecessary at all, and there is no repetition in the statement. Faith and righteous deeds did not begin only with this ummah; believers and righteous people had also lived before. How, then, without adding the word *minkum,* could a perfect distinction have been made? If the verse had just read, [1] وَعَدَ اللّٰهُ الَّذِيْنَ آمَنُوْا وَعَمِلُوْا الصَّالِحٰتِ [Allah has promised to those who believe and do good works] the identity of the righteous mentioned in the verse would have remained unclear as to whether they are from among this ummah or the previous ones. And if only the word مِنْكُمْ **[*minkum*—from among you]** was there without being accompanied by الَّذِيْنَ آمَنُوْا وَعَمِلُوْا الصَّالِحٰتِ [those who believe and do good works] it would have been taken to mean that even the sinful and wicked people could become *Khulafā',* whereas the fact is that the rule of the sinful is only by way of trial and not by way of exaltation. Only righteous believers and doers of good deeds are true *Khulafā'* of God Almighty, whether spiritual or worldly.

There is a misconception that, as generally understood, the last part of this verse, i.e. [2] وَمَنْ كَفَرَ بَعْدَ ذٰلِكَ فَاُولٰٓئِكَ هُمُ الْفٰسِقُوْنَ [then whoso

1. Without the word *minkum,* the hypothetical verse can be read as so: 'Allah promised to those who believed and did good works.' [Publisher]

2. *Sūrah an-Nūr,* 24:56 [Publisher]

is ungrateful after that, they will be the rebellious] is meaningless. This idea is so absurd that it is laughable. For, the clear and plain meaning of this verse is that Allah the Glorious, after giving glad tidings of the appearance of the *Khulafā',* warns the rebels and the disobedient that after the appearance of *Khulafā'*—who will appear from time to time—if someone rebelled and did not obey and pledge allegiance to them, he will be considered rebellious.

How then is the [last part of the] verse meaningless? Clearly, this verse is in line with the following hadith of the Holy Prophet, peace and blessings of Allah be upon him: مَنْ لَمْ يَعْرِفْ إِمَامَ زَمَانِهِ فَقَدْ مَاتَ مِيتَةَ الْجَاهِلِيَّةِ; [whosoever does not recognize the Imam of his age shall die the death of ignorance]. Meaning that, Imams will appear in every age and those who do not recognize them, their death will resemble the death of the disbelievers. It is pointless for the critic to present the following verse and to conclude that here the word مِنْكُمْ [*minkum*—from among you] is meant exclusively for those who were present at that time:

قَالَ اللّٰهُ اِنِّيْ مُنَزِّلُهَا عَلَيْكُمْ فَمَنْ يَّكْفُرْ بَعْدُ مِنْكُمْ فَاِنِّيْٓ اُعَذِّبُهٗ عَذَابًا لَّآ اُعَذِّبُهٗٓ اَحَدًا مِّنَ الْعٰلَمِيْنَ[1]

As I have already pointed out it is a common way of expression in the Holy Quran, and is used very frequently in it, that its address is general and its commandments are meant for the whole of the ummah, and are not exclusive to the Companions[ra]. Of course,

1. Allah said, 'Surely, I will send it down to you, but whosoever from among you disbelieves afterwards—I will surely punish them with a punishment wherewith I will not punish any other of the peoples' (*Sūrah al-Mā'idah,* 5:116). [Publisher]

there are places where there is a clear context indicating that the address is specific. Such places are exceptions. Accordingly, in the above-mentioned verse, a particular group of the apostles asked for a meal and they alone were addressed. So this evidence is enough that only that group was addressed that asked the question. But to say that there are numerous such examples in the Holy Quran is a complete lie and deception. The word *minkum* has been used around eighty-two times in the Holy Quran and there are nearly 600 examples of address in other forms, but all the addresses in which commandments are given have a general application.

If the Quranic commandments were meant exclusively for the Companions[ra], the Holy Quran would have become redundant upon their death. In fact, the verse at issue, which is about *Khilāfat,* really resembles the following verse:

لَهُمُ الْبُشْرٰى فِى الْحَيٰوةِ الدُّنْيَا[1]

Were these glad tidings exclusively for the Companions[ra], or might someone else, too, partake of them? The critic insists that whosoever departs from the 'true interpretation,' i.e. makes a broad application of the Quranic commandments meant for their direct addressees, must support his departure with some categorical argument. This proves that the critic is not only totally unaware of the style of the Holy Quran, but also that of all Divine Books. The trouble is that hasty people are quite ready to object before thoroughly investigating the matter. Had the critic

1. For them are glad tidings in the present life (*Sūrah Yūnus,* 10:65). [Publisher]

wished to investigate with honest intent, he should have pondered over all the places where apparently only the Companion are addressed. And then he should have studied as to what was the most frequent, probable, and unqualified usage of the Holy Quran. Because the true meaning would be determined clearly in light of the most standard usage and—unless there is a qualifying context—deviation from them would be impermissible.

Let it be clear that the Holy Quran's basic style of address is general. This is why 600 commandments of the Holy Quran are considered to be applicable to everyone, and not limited only to the Companions. So, if someone departs from this basic style of the Holy Quran and thinks that a particular commandment is limited to the Companions, to the exclusion of others, the burden of proof is on that person. For example, Allah, the Lord of Glory, apparently addresses the Companions alone in the Holy Quran, saying:

1. Worship God alone;
2. Seek His help with perseverance and prayer;
3. Eat only of pure things;
4. Do not create any kind of disorder;
5. Give zakat and
6. Offer Prayer;
7. Take the station of Abraham as a place of prayer;
8. Vie with each other in good deeds;
9. Remember Me, I will remember you;
10. Be grateful to Me;
11. Pray to Me;

12. Do not regard those who are martyred in the way of God as dead;
13. Do not give the name of disbeliever and faithless to the one who conveys greetings of peace to you;
14. Eat of the pure things from the earth;
15. Do not follow Satan;
16. Fasting has been prescribed for you;
17. But whoso among you is sick or on journey shall fast the same number of other days;
18. Do not devour each other's wealth unjustly;
19. Be righteous so that you may prosper;
20. Fight in the cause of God against those who fight against you;
21. But do not exceed the limit;
22. And do not transgress as God loves not the transgressors;
23. Spend in the way of God;
24. Cast not yourself into ruin with your own hands;
25. Do good to others because Allah loves those who do good to others;
26. Complete the hajj and umrah for the sake of Allah;
27. Furnish yourself with provisions because there is a benefit in it that you will not have to beg others; this means that begging is a disgrace and one should make plans to avoid it;
28. Enter Islam and peace;
29. Marry not idolatrous women until they believe;
30. And O believing women! Marry not idolaters until they believe;

31. And send something ahead for yourselves;
32. Make not God a target for your oaths;
33. Do not detain women to make them suffer;
34. And those of you who die, their widows must not marry for four months and ten days;
35. If you divorce women, then send them away in a becoming manner;
36. If you are in a state of fear, then say your prayer on foot or riding;
37. If you give alms openly, it is, generally speaking, beneficial as people may emulate your good deeds; but if you give in secret and to the poor, it is better for you;
38. When you lend someone some money, write it down; and
39. Fear God with regard to paying your debts and do not leave any sum unpaid;
40. And have witnesses when you sell or buy something;
41. And if you be on a journey, and you find not a scribe, then let there be a pledge with possession;
42. And hold fast, all together, to the rope of Allah and be not divided;
43. And let there be among you a body of men who should invite to goodness, enjoin equity, and forbid evil;
44. Rush towards the forgiveness of Allah;
45. If someone's wife dies, he shall have half of that which she leaves, if she has no child;
46. But if she has a child, then he shall have a fourth of that which she leaves, after the payment of any bequests.

I have written these commandments by way of example. Even a person with a modicum of reason can realize that, although apparently only the Companions[ra] are addressed, in fact, all Muslims, and not just the Companions[ra], are obligated to act upon these injunctions. In short, the true and real Quranic style that generally characterizes the Holy Quran is that its real addressees are all the Muslims who will be born until doomsday, even though, apparently, only the Companions of the Holy Prophet[sas] are being addressed. Hence, if someone claims that this promise or warning was limited to the Companions[ra], he deviates from the common Quranic expression. Until he substantiates his claim with conclusive proof, he will be considered a *mulḥid* [atheist] for taking such a stance. Was the Holy Quran revealed only for the Companions[ra]? If the promises, warnings, and all the commandments of the Holy Quran were restricted to the Companions[ra], then those born afterwards would have nothing to do with the Holy Quran. نَعُوْذُ بِاللّٰهِ مِنْ هٰذِهِ الْخُرَافَاتِ [We seek refuge with Allah from such absurdities].

To allege that, according to a hadith, *Khilāfat* will last only thirty years is inexplicable. The Holy Quran says,

ثُلَّةٌ مِّنَ الْاَوَّلِيْنَ ۝ وَ ثُلَّةٌ مِّنَ الْاٰخِرِيْنَ ۝[1]

Therefore, how absurd is it to present any hadith against it and to interpret the hadith to mean what is obviously contrary to the Holy Quran? If the account of *aḥādīth* is to be relied upon, then

1. A large party from among the early *Muslims,* and a large party from the later ones (*Sūrah al-Wāqi'ah,* 56:40–41). [Publisher]

those *aḥādīth* that are much more authentic and trustworthy than this hadith should be accepted first; e.g. those *aḥādīth* of *Ṣaḥīḥ al-Bukhārī* foretelling the appearance of *Khulafā'* in the Latter Days, especially that *khalīfah* about whom it is recorded in *Ṣaḥīḥ al-Bukhārī* that, for him, a voice will descend from heaven: هٰذَا خَلِيْفَةُ اللهِ الْمَهْدِيّ [This is God's *Khalīfah,* the Guided One]. Now consider the status and credibility of this hadith—which is recorded in the most authentic of books after the Book of Allah. On the other hand, the hadith that has been presented by the critic has been criticized by the ulema on many grounds and its authenticity has been questioned. Has this critic not pondered over the prophecies regarding the appearance of certain *Khulafā'* in the Latter Days that 'a *ḥārith*[1] will come; the Mahdi will appear; a heavenly *khalīfah* will come. Are they recorded in the books of *aḥādīth* or in some other book?

It is established from *aḥādīth* that there are three periods [after the Holy Prophet[sas]]: first, the period of the Rightly Guided *Khilāfat;* then, a period of great chaos when tyrant kings would rule. Then there would be the final period, which would resemble the period of Prophethood, so much so that the Holy Prophet, peace and blessings of Allah be upon him, said that the first and last period of my ummah bear great resemblance to each other; these two periods are like a rain filled with such goodness and blessings that no one knows whether the first part is more blessed or the latter.

1. Lit. 'a cultivator of land', or 'one who gathers'. A title for the Latter Days Messenger. [Publisher]

Let it also be clear that Allah, the Lord of Glory, says in the Holy Quran:

إِنَّا نَحْنُ نَزَّلْنَا الذِّكْرَ وَإِنَّا لَهُ لَحٰفِظُوْنَ[1]

Meaning that, it is We who have sent down this Book and most surely We will safeguard this revelation.

This verse contains the proclamation that this Word is everlasting, and there will always appear such people who shall revive its teachings and deliver its benefits to the people. And if it is asked, what is the benefit of the continued existence of the Holy Quran—and its true safeguarding, too, rests upon the existence of this benefit—then another verse makes it clear:

هُوَ الَّذِىْ بَعَثَ فِى الْاُمِّيّٖنَ رَسُوْلًا مِّنْهُمْ يَتْلُوْا عَلَيْهِمْ اٰيٰتِهٖ وَ يُزَكِّيْهِمْ وَ يُعَلِّمُهُمُ الْكِتٰبَ وَ الْحِكْمَةَ[2]

The gist of this verse is that the Holy Quran has two great purposes, for the achieving of which the Holy Prophet, peace and blessings of Allah be upon him, came: The first is the wisdom of the Holy Quran; that is to say, its insights and fine points; and the second is the effect of the Holy Quran, which purifies the souls.

The safeguarding of the Quran does not merely mean that its text should be preserved, for the Jews and Christians also

1. *Sūrah al-Ḥijr,* 15:10 [Publisher]

2. He it is who has raised among the unlettered *people* a Messenger from among themselves who recites unto them His Signs, and purifies them, and teaches them the Book and wisdom, although they had been, before, in manifest misguidance (*Sūrah al-Jumu'ah,* 62:3). [Publisher]

performed this function in the early ages with respect to their scriptures, so much so that even the dots contained in the Torah were calculated. Rather, the safeguarding of the Holy Quran means both the safeguarding of the text and the safeguarding of the benefits and effects of the Quran. And, in accord with divine practice, this can be done only if from time to time deputies of the Holy Prophet, peace and blessings of Allah be upon him, appear who should enjoy all the bounties of Messengership by way of *ẓill* [reflection], and who should be bestowed all the blessings that are bestowed upon the Prophets. This magnificent purpose is indicated in the verse:

وَعَدَ اللّٰهُ الَّذِيْنَ اٰمَنُوْا مِنْكُمْ وَ عَمِلُوا الصّٰلِحٰتِ لَيَسْتَخْلِفَنَّهُمْ فِي الْاَرْضِ كَمَا اسْتَخْلَفَ الَّذِيْنَ
مِنْ قَبْلِهِمْ وَ لَيُمَكِّنَنَّ لَهُمْ دِيْنَهُمُ الَّذِي ارْتَضٰى لَهُمْ وَ لَيُبَدِّلَنَّهُمْ مِّنْ بَعْدِ خَوْفِهِمْ اَمْنًا ؕ
يَعْبُدُوْنَنِيْ لَا يُشْرِكُوْنَ بِيْ شَيْـًٔا ؕ وَمَنْ كَفَرَ بَعْدَ ذٰلِكَ فَاُولٰٓئِكَ هُمُ الْفٰسِقُوْنَ [1]

In fact, this verse serves to elaborate the meanings of the other verse:

اِنَّا نَحْنُ نَزَّلْنَا الذِّكْرَ وَ اِنَّا لَهٗ لَحٰفِظُوْنَ [2]

1. Allah has promised to those among you who believe and do good works that He will surely make them Successors in the earth, as He made Successors *from among* those who were before them; and that He will surely establish for them their religion which He has chosen for them; and that He will surely give them in exchange security and peace after their fear: They will worship Me, and they will not associate anything with Me. Then whoso is ungrateful after that, they will be the rebellious (*Sūrah an-Nūr,* 24:56). [Publisher]

2. Verily, We Ourself have sent down this Exhortation, and most surely We will be its Guardian (*Sūrah al-Ḥijr,* 15:10). [Publisher]

It answers the question as to how and by what means the Holy Quran will be safeguarded. In this regard, God Almighty says that He will continue sending *Khulafā'* of this Holy Prophet, peace and blessings of Allah be upon him, from time to time. And the word *khalīfah* has been chosen to imply that they will be successors to the Holy Prophet, peace and blessings of Allah be upon him, and will partake of his blessings, as occurred in earlier times. They will spread the Faith and establish peace after fear; that is, they will appear at such times as when Islam will be rife with schisms. And whosoever defies them after their coming will be depraved and rebellious. This is the answer to the ignorant one who asks: Is it obligatory for us to believe in the *Auliyā'*? Allah the Exalted says, indeed, it is obligatory, and those who oppose them and die while opposing them are the rebellious.

In this context, the critic has also written that God Almighty has said:

اَلْيَوْمَ اَكْمَلْتُ لَكُمْ دِيْنَكُمْ وَ اَتْمَمْتُ عَلَيْكُمْ نِعْمَتِيْ[1]

Then, the critic asserts that since the Religion has been perfected, and the favours have been completed, therefore, no *Mujaddid* or Prophet is now needed. Sadly, the critic has raised an objection against the Holy Quran itself by such thinking, inasmuch as the Holy Quran has promised the appointment of *Khulafā'* from the ummah, as has been mentioned earlier, and has said that through them the Religion will be strengthened, doubts will be put to rest and, following after a state of fear, security will be

1. This day have I perfected your religion for you and completed My favour upon you (*Sūrah al-Mā'idah,* 5:4). [Publisher]

restored. Thus, if nothing is permissible after the perfection of the Religion, then, according to the statement of this critic, the thirty years of *Khilāfat* [after the Holy Prophet[sas]] would also be rendered unnecessary, as the Religion had been perfected and nothing more was needed.

In fact, it is out of place for the uninformed critic to cite the verse:

اَلْيَوْمَ اَكْمَلْتُ لَكُمْ دِيْنَكُمْ [1]

When do we allege that a *Mujaddid* or *Muḥaddath* subtracts anything from the Faith or adds anything to it? Rather, our position is that when, after the lapse of time, the dust of faulty thinking covers the holy teaching of the Faith and the pure countenance of truth becomes hidden, then *Mujaddidīn, Muḥaddathīn,* and spiritual *Khulafā'* appear to reveal the true and beautiful countenance of the Faith. We do not know whence our hopeless critic has learnt that *Mujaddidīn* and spiritual *Khulafā'* arrive with the purpose of changing or abrogating the Faith. No, they do not come to abrogate the Faith, but to display the light and brilliance of the Faith.

The critic's position that there is no such need reveals that he does not have much regard for the Faith. He has never reflected on what Islam is, what its progress signifies, how and in what manner its real progress can be achieved, and who can be considered a true Muslim. That is why the critic considers it enough that—the Holy

1. This day have I perfected your religion for you (*Sūrah al-Mā'idah,* 5:4). [Publisher]

Quran being available, and there being a plethora of ulema—the hearts of most people are drawn automatically to Islam and no *Mujaddid* is needed. It is a pity, however, that he does not appreciate the fact that *Mujaddidīn* and spiritual *Khulafā'* are needed in this ummah in the same way that, from ancient times, the need for Prophets kept presenting itself.

It cannot be denied that Ḥaḍrat Mūsā [Moses], peace be on him, was a Prophet and a Messenger, and that the Torah was a complete code for the Children of Israel. And just as the Holy Quran contains the verse, اَلْيَوْمَ اَكْمَلْتُ لَكُمْ[1] so does the Torah contain verses to the effect that the Children of Israel have been given a perfect and glorious Book, the name of which is the Torah. The Holy Quran also describes the Torah as such. Yet, after the Torah, hundreds of Prophets appeared among the Children of Israel. They brought no new Book and their purpose was to draw people who had departed from the teachings of the Torah back to it, and to purify the hearts of those who had been afflicted with doubts, atheism, and a lack of faith. Allah, the Lord of Glory, Himself affirms it in the Holy Quran:

وَلَقَدْ اٰتَيْنَا مُوْسَى الْكِتٰبَ وَقَفَّيْنَا مِنْۢ بَعْدِهٖ بِالرُّسُلِ[2]

Meaning that, We bestowed the Torah upon Moses and after that Book, We sent many Messengers in its support and to testify to its truth.

1. This day have I perfected your religion for you (*Sūrah al-Mā'idah,* 5:4). [Publisher]

2. *Sūrah al-Baqarah,* 2:88 [Publisher]

Similarly, Allah says in another place:

ثُمَّ اَرْسَلْنَا رُسُلَنَا تَتْرَا[1]

Meaning that, then, We sent Our Messengers one after the other.

All these verses show that it is the way of Allah that after sending down His Book, He definitely sends Prophets in support of it. Accordingly, in support of the Torah, sometimes as many as 400 Prophets were sent at one and the same time, to which the Bible testifies to this day.

The underlying reason for sending so many Messengers is that God Almighty has warned emphatically that whoever denies His true Book shall endure in hell as punishment, as He says:

The reason for sending so many Messengers is that God Almighty has warned emphatically that whoever denies His true Book shall abide in hell is the punishment for the denial, as He says:

وَالَّذِيْنَ كَفَرُوْا وَكَذَّبُوْا بِاٰيٰتِنَآ اُولٰٓئِكَ اَصْحٰبُ النَّارِ ۚ هُمْ فِيْهَا خٰلِدُوْنَ[2]

Meaning that, those who disbelieved and rejected Our Signs are condemned to the Fire and shall abide therein forever.

Thus, according to the Divine Book, the punishment for rejection is very severe; but on the other hand, the issue of Prophethood and divine revelation is also very subtle. Indeed God Almighty is Himself so Transcendent that it is impossible

1. *Sūrah al-Mu'minūn*, 23:45 [Publisher]

2. *Sūrah al-Baqarah,* 2:40 [Publisher]

to achieve His true and holy cognition—let alone the comprehension of Prophets and Divine Books—unless divine light illuminates the human eye. Therefore, the *raḥmāniyyat* [graciousness] of God demanded that His blind and unseeing creatures should be helped greatly. And that the disbelievers should not be committed to the everlasting torment of hell on account of the denial of such doctrines after sending a Messenger and a Book once, even though after the passage of a long time, the later generations could not understand them to be any more than pious and commendable statements.

In fact, it should be clear and evident to a rational person: How can God, who is *Raḥmān* [Gracious] and *Raḥīm* [Merciful], prescribe so great a punishment as condemnation to everlasting hell for peoples of different nations who have heard of the Quran and the Messenger after many centuries, and who, not being proficient in Arabic, cannot understand the excellences of the Holy Quran. Nor can the conscience of any human being accept that a person may be condemned without being provided convincing arguments that the Holy Quran is the Word of God. That is why God Almighty has promised to continue to appoint *Khulafā'* so that, being invested with the light of Prophethood by way of *ẓill,* they may demonstrate the excellences of the Holy Quran and its holy blessings to the people, thus making them accountable. It should also be remembered that in every age such a conclusive argument assumes different forms, and that the *Mujaddid* of the time is equipped with the faculties, capacities, and qualities suited to reform the mischief of that time. Thus, God Almighty will continue to do so as long as He wills, so that reform and virtue may continue to flourish. And these statements are not unsubstantiated; in fact, an unbroken series of precedents testifies to them.

And apart from the Prophets, Messengers, and *Muḥaddathīn* who appeared at different times in different countries, if one were to examine only those Prophets, Messengers, and *Muḥaddathīn* who appeared among the Children of Israel, it would be discovered that during the 1,400 years between Moses and Jesus, thousands of Prophets and *Muḥaddathīn* appeared and diligently occupied themselves in the service of the Torah. The Holy Quran and the Bible both testify to this. Those Prophets brought no new book and taught no new faith. They served only the Torah. They appeared whenever atheism, disbelief, misconduct, and hard-heartedness became prevalent among the Children of Israel.

A rational person ought to consider that although the Law of Moses was limited in its scope and was not meant for the whole of mankind, nor was it to last forever, God Almighty nevertheless took care to send thousands of Prophets for the revival of that law, and they exhibited such Signs as enabled the Children of Israel to behold God afresh. How, then, can it be that Muslims—who have been designated as the best of people, and are attached to the Best of the Messengers, peace and blessings of Allah be upon him—be accounted so unfortunate that God Almighty looked upon them with mercy for only thirty years, and after showing them heavenly light during that period, turned His Face away from them? Centuries passed after the departure of the Holy Prophet, and thousands of disorders arose, and great earthquakes were felt, and diverse forms of corruption spread, and a whole world mounted attacks against Islam, and all its blessings and miracles were denied and declared unacceptable.

And yet, God Almighty never looked upon the Muslims nor had mercy on them, nor did He consider that the Muslims were also weak human beings and, like the Children of Israel, their plants also were in need of heavenly water. Could the Beneficent God, who sent the Holy Prophet, peace and blessings of Allah be upon him, to remove all corruption forever, turn away from the Muslims like this? Can we imagine that God Almighty was so merciful towards previous peoples and—having revealed the Torah—sent thousands of Prophets and *Muḥaddathīn* in support of the Torah and for the repeated revival of the hearts of the Children of Israel, but that the Muslims were subject to His wrath and, therefore, after the revelation of the Holy Quran, He forgot them and left their religious scholars forever to their personal judgement and innovations? Concerning Ḥaḍrat Mūsā, God said clearly:

وَكَلَّمَ اللّٰهُ مُوْسٰى تَكْلِيْمًا ○ رُسُلًا مُّبَشِّرِيْنَ وَمُنْذِرِيْنَ لِئَلَّا يَكُوْنَ لِلنَّاسِ عَلَى اللّٰهِ حُجَّةٌ بَعْدَ الرُّسُلِ ۚ وَكَانَ اللّٰهُ عَزِيْزًا حَكِيْمًا ○[1]

Meaning that, God spoke to Ḥaḍrat Mūsā and sent Messengers bearing glad tidings as well as warnings to help him and to testify to his truth, so that people may not have any excuse after that, and, having witnessed a series of Prophets, should believe in the Torah with all their heart. Moreover, He says:

وَرُسُلًا قَدْ قَصَصْنٰهُمْ عَلَيْكَ مِنْ قَبْلُ وَرُسُلًا لَّمْ نَقْصُصْهُمْ عَلَيْكَ [2]

1. *Sūrah an-Nisā',* 4:165–166 [Publisher]

2. *Sūrah an-Nisā',* 4:165 [Publisher]

Meaning that, We sent many Messengers before you, some of whom We have mentioned to you and some We have not mentioned.

Could it be that He did not make any such arrangement for the Muslims and withheld from them the mercy and grace He had bestowed upon the people of Ḥaḍrat Mūsā?

It is obvious that, with the passage of time, previous miracles and wonders became mere tales. Succeeding generations, finding themselves bereft of all such wonders, begin to entertain doubts about miracles and extraordinary happenings. Having the example of thousands of Prophets of Israel before them, the Muslims would be disheartened and, considering themselves unfortunate, would either envy the Children of Israel or would consider the history of Israel, too, to be a chain of imaginary tales.

It is futile to assert that, as there have been thousands of Prophets and many miracles have been shown in the past, the Muslims were in no need of extraordinary events and wonders and blessings, and that is why God Almighty held back everything of that kind from the Muslims. Those who have no regard for the Faith make this kind of assertion. Man is very weak and remains in need of his faith being strengthened. In this respect, no help can be derived from self-conceived arguments. It is necessary to realize afresh that God exists. However, false belief, which is not effective in restraining a person from misconduct, may continue to exist as a matter of inherited stories or traditions.

It should also be remembered here that the perfection of faith does not dispense with the need for safeguarding it. For example, a person builds a house, sets all its rooms in order, and fulfils all the requirements relating to its structure; but after a long time, dust settles on it, and because of rains and dust storms, its beauty is concealed. It would be the height of folly to stop a person who inherits this house from undertaking its cleaning and whitewash because the house was completed long ago.

It is a pity that people who make such critiques do not reflect that the completion of a structure is one thing and its periodic cleaning is quite another. It should be remembered that Reformers do not add anything to or subtract anything from the Faith. They restore to the hearts that which had been lost. And it is disobedience of a divine command to assert that it is not necessary to believe in *Mujaddidīn,* because God Almighty has directed:

وَمَنْ كَفَرَ بَعْدَ ذٰلِكَ فَاُولٰٓئِكَ هُمُ الْفٰسِقُوْنَ[1]

Meaning that, whoever rejects the *Khulafā'* who will be sent thereafter is indeed from amongst the sinners.

I will now summarize this subject as follows. The arguments that have been presented below prove that it was necessary that after the death of the Messenger of Allah, peace and blessings of Allah be upon him, Reformers should have appeared among the Muslims at times of disorder and trials. They would be entrusted with one of the functions of the Prophets; namely, that they would call to the true Faith and remove all innovations that have been intermingled with it. Being equipped with the heavenly light, they would exhibit the truth of the Faith from every point

1. *Sūrah an-Nūr,* 24:56 [Publisher]

of view and invite people to truth, love, and piety by the force of their example. The arguments for this are:

FIRST—Reason affirms that matters relating to God and the Hereafter are very subtle and conceptual, namely, one has to believe in matters of the unseen and beyond the realm of rationalization. No one has ever seen God Almighty or observed Heaven and Hell, or met the angels. Moreover, divine commandments are opposed to the desires of the ego and restrain from that in which the ego delights. Therefore, reason dictates that it is not only appropriate, rather it is essential, that either the Prophets of God, who bring the law and the Book and possess spiritual power, should live long and continue to bless their followers in each century with their company, and should train them under their own graceful supervision and convey to them the blessing, light, and spiritual insights that they had provided in the early part of their ministry; or, if that should not be possible, then their spiritual heirs, who are equipped with their high qualities and can set forth the verities and insights comprised in the Divine Book, under the guidance of revelation, and can illustrate in practice that which is related to the past and can lead a seeker after truth to certainty, must continue to appear in times of trouble and trials so that those afflicted with doubt and forgetfulness should not be deprived of the true grace of the Prophets.

It is obvious that when the time of a Prophet comes to an end, and those who have witnessed his blessings also pass away, their experiences become tales in the eyes of the people of the next generation. The moral qualities of the Prophet, his worship, his steadfastness, his devotion, divine support, extraordinary events, and miracles which testified to his Prophethood and the truth of his claim become fictions in the estimation of subsequent generations. Therefore, the freshness of the faith and the eagerness of obedience that are the characteristics of those who are favoured with the company of the Prophet are not found in those who come after them.

It is clear that in the centuries that followed, no example can be found of the kind of fortitude of faith shown by the Companions of the Holy Prophet, may peace and blessings of Allah be upon him, and the utmost sincerity with which they sacrificed their wealth, lives, and honour in the cause of Islam. Indeed it is not found even in the second century itself, that is to say, among the *Tābi'īn.*[1] What was the reason for this? It was certainly because the Companions, may Allah be pleased with them, had beheld the countenance of that true one, whose being the lover for Allah was so spontaneously testified to even by the disbelieving Quraish. These people, observing his daily supplications, his loving prostrations, his condition of complete obedience, the bright signs of perfect love and devotion on his countenance, and witnessing divine light raining down upon his face, were compelled to say that: عَشِقَ مُحَمَّدٌ عَلٰى رَبِّهٖ Meaning that, Muhammad[ṣas] is passionately in love with his Lord.

Moreover, the Companions observed not only that devotion, love, and sincerity, but matching this love—which surged up in the heart of our lord and master Muhammad, peace and blessings

1. The *Tābi'īn* are the generation of Muslims who met or saw the blessed Companions[ra] of the Holy Prophet[ṣas] but not the Prophet[ṣas] himself. [Publisher]

of Allah be on him, like a raging ocean—they also observed God Almighty's love for him, in the form of extraordinary support and help. Thus they realized that God exists, and their hearts testified aloud that God is with this man. They saw divine wonders to such an extent and witnessed heavenly Signs to such a degree that they were left with no doubt whatsoever that there does, indeed, exist a Supreme Being whose name is God, who controls everything and for whom nothing is impossible. That is indeed why they exhibited such deeds of devotion and sincerity and made such sacrifices as are not possible for anyone to perform until all doubts and suspicions have been removed. They saw with their own eyes that the pleasure of that Holy Being lies only in embracing Islam and adopting the obedience of His Noble Messenger[sas] with heart and soul. After this absolute certainty, the kind of obedience that they exhibited and the feats they performed and the manner in which they laid down their lives at the feet of their holy guide, were matters that were not possible for anyone who had not witnessed the blossoming spectacle that the Companions witnessed.

Such high qualities cannot be developed without these means, and salvation cannot be truly achieved without witnessing such excellences. It is, therefore, necessary that God the Benevolent, who has invited everyone to salvation, should make a similar arrangement in every century so that His creatures should not fail in any age to attain the stages of absolute certainty.

To say that the Holy Quran and the *aḥādīth* alone suffice us, and we do not need the company of the righteous, is itself opposed to the teachings of the Holy Quran, as Allah, the Lord of Glory, says:

وَ كُوْنُوْا مَعَ الصّٰدِقِيْنَ[1]

The truthful are those who have recognized the truth through their spiritual insight and are wholeheartedly devoted to it. This high grade of spiritual insight cannot be achieved unless heavenly guidance conveys a seeker to the highest stage of absolute certainty. In this sense, the truly righteous are the Prophets, the Messengers, the *Muḥaddathīn,* and the perfect and consummate *Auliyā'* upon whom heavenly light descended and who beheld God Almighty with the sight of certainty in this very world. The verse that we have just quoted indicates that the world is never left without the truthful, as the perpetual commandment وَ كُوْنُوْا مَعَ الصّٰدِقِيْنَ[2] necessitates the presence of the truthful at all times.

Besides, observation indicates clearly that those people who spend their lives without any care for keeping the company of the righteous are certainly not able to cleanse themselves of their physical passions through their learning and skills. Indeed, they fail to attain even that minimum status in Islam that generates the certainty of belief in the existence of God. They surely do not have the same certainty about God Almighty that they have about their wealth, which is locked in their boxes, or about the houses that they own. They are afraid of consuming arsenic because they know for certain that it is a fatal poison, but they are not afraid of the poison of sin, though they read in the Holy Quran every day:

1. And be with the truthful (*Sūrah at-Taubah,* 9:119). [Publisher]
2. *Sūrah at-Taubah,* 9:119 [Publisher]

إِنَّهُۥ مَن يَأْتِ رَبَّهُۥ مُجْرِمًا فَإِنَّ لَهُۥ جَهَنَّمَ ۖ لَا يَمُوتُ فِيهَا وَلَا يَحْيَىٰ[1]

Thus the truth is that the person who does not recognize God Almighty can also not recognize the Holy Quran. Of course, it is also true that the Holy Quran has been revealed for guidance, but the guidance of the Quran is bound up with the being of that person upon whom the Quran was revealed or that person whom Allah appoints as his deputy.

Had the Quran been sufficient by itself, God Almighty had the power to have the Quran inscribed through natural means on the leaves of trees or have it descend from heaven written out fully; but God Almighty did not do so. In fact, He did not send the Quran into the world until the teacher of the Quran had been sent. Open the Noble Quran and see how many verses there are where the Holy Quran addresses this subject:

يُعَلِّمُهُمُ الْكِتٰبَ وَالْحِكْمَةَ[2]

Meaning, that Noble Prophet, peace and blessings of Allah be upon him, teaches the Quran and Quranic wisdom to the people. And then at one place it further states:

لَا يَمَسُّهٗٓ اِلَّا الْمُطَهَّرُوْنَ[3]

1. Verily, he who comes to his Lord a sinner—for him is Hell; he shall neither die therein nor live (*Sūrah Ṭā Hā,* 20:75). [Publisher]

2. *Sūrah al-Jumu'ah,* 62:3 [Publisher]

3. *Sūrah al-Wāqi'ah,* 56:80 [Publisher]

Meaning that, the verities and deep insights of the Quran are revealed only to those who have been purified. These verses prove clearly that in order to understand the Quran such a teacher is needed whom God Almighty has purified with His own Hand. Had there not been the need for a teacher to learn the Quran, there would not have been any such need in the beginning of this period either.

It is futile to assert that a teacher was needed in the beginning for the resolution of the difficult parts of the Quran, but once those difficulties had been resolved, there is no need for a teacher now. The answer to this is that even matters that have been resolved are in need of further resolution after a time. Apart from this, the Muslim ummah also faces new difficulties in every age; and while it is indeed true that the Quran comprises all knowledge, it is not necessary that all its knowledge should have been disclosed in one period alone. On the contrary, as various types of difficulties are faced, so are those types of Quranic knowledge revealed.

In accord with the difficulties faced in every age, spiritual teachers, who are the heirs of the Messengers and are invested with their qualities by way of *ẓill,* are sent to resolve those difficulties. And the *Mujaddid* whose functions have a strong resemblance with the official activities of a specific Messenger, bears the name of that Messenger in the estimation of Allah.

The need for new teachers arises also because some portions of the teaching of the Holy Quran need to be set out by example and cannot be confined to mere verbal explanation. The Holy Prophet, peace and blessings of Allah be upon him, who was the first teacher and the true heir of this throne, made his Companions[ra] understand these fine points by his own living example. For example, God Almighty stating that I am the Knower of the unseen and that I am the One who responds to those who call upon Me, and am All-Powerful, and the One who accepts prayers, and leads seekers to the true light, and sends down revelation upon My sincere servants, and causes My spirit to descend upon whomsoever of My servants as I wish—these are all matters that can never be understood until the teacher demonstrates them as an exemplar himself.

Thus it is clear that those who are scholars only in name, who are themselves blind, cannot make the people understand these teachings. On the contrary, they constantly create doubts in the minds of their disciples concerning the greatness of Islam and say that all these matters relate not to the future but have been left behind and can no longer be experienced. It is understood from such statements of theirs as if Islam is no longer a living faith and that there is now absolutely no way to attain to its true teachings. It is obvious, however, that if it is the will of God Almighty to make His creatures always drink water from the spring of the Holy Quran, He would without doubt have made provisions for it in accordance with His eternal practice. Had the teachings of the Holy Quran been limited to the same extent to which the teaching of an experienced and fine-thinking philosopher is limited, and did not comprise the heavenly teaching that can be demonstrated only by practice, then, God forbid, the revelation of the Quran was unnecessary. But I know that if one were to reflect even for a moment upon this issue—as to the distinction between the teaching of the Prophets and the teaching of the philosophers, assuming the soundness of both teachings—the only distinction that would be discovered is that a great portion of the teaching of the Prophets is beyond the reach of human intellect and can be understood and appreciated only through practical demonstration, and can be imbued into the hearts only by those who have experienced them personally.

For example, matters such as how the angels take a soul; how they take it to the heavens; how one is taken to account in the grave; what is the nature of Paradise, Hell, and the bridge of *Ṣirāṭ;* the fact that four angels are holding up the throne of Allah and that on the Day of Resurrection it will be eight; and the way God sends revelation to His servants and how He blesses them with divine visions—all these are spiritual phenomena that cannot be grasped through mere talk.

This being the case, I say again that if Allah, the Lord of Glory, has so willed that this portion of the teaching of His Book should not be confined to the early ages, then without doubt He must have arranged also for the teachers of that portion to be available at all times, since the portion of the teaching which relates to personal experience can certainly not be comprehended except through teachers who have experienced it.

The people stumble at minor and insignificant issues. Therefore if, after the Holy Prophet, peace and blessings of Allah be upon him, such teachers did not come in Islam, who possessed the light of Prophethood by way of *ẓill,* it would appear that God Almighty deliberately allowed the Quran to become useless, since those who understood the Holy Quran truly and correctly were taken away from the world at a very early stage. But this would be contrary to His promise, as He says:

إِنَّا نَحْنُ نَزَّلْنَا الذِّكْرَ وَإِنَّا لَهُ لَحٰفِظُوْنَ[1]

Meaning that, it is We who have sent down the Quran and We shall continue to safeguard it.

Now, I am unable to understand—supposing that there remain none from among those who understand the Holy Quran, and those who believe in it with certainty based on personal experience have all passed into oblivion—how has the Quran been safeguarded? Does safeguarding it mean that the Quran, beautifully inscribed, would be preserved forever locked in boxes like certain treasures—buried safely under the earth, but of no use to anyone? Can anyone imagine that this is the intent of God Almighty by this verse? If this indeed is the intent, then such safeguarding is no excellence at all. Rather, such a claim is laughable and mentioning such safeguarding would invite ridicule from the enemies. Because when the actual purpose is not achieved, then what benefit can there be from mere verbal safeguarding.

It is possible that some copy of the Gospel or the Torah may similarly be found preserved in some pit. Moreover, thousands of books are found in the world, which are understood to be the composition of some author without any alteration. So what excellence is there in such safeguarding and what benefit can it bestow upon the ummah.

It is true that the safeguarding of the text of the Holy Quran is greater than that of all other books in the world and is miraculous, but we certainly cannot imagine that the Being of God Almighty, who always has spiritual objectives in sight, desired the

1. *Sūrah al-Ḥijr,* 15:10 [Publisher]

safeguarding of just the literal wording of the Holy Quran. The very word ذِكْر [*Dhikr*—remembrance][1] indicates clearly that the Holy Quran will be preserved forever as a remembrance, and its true *dhākirs* [those who engage in remembrance] will always be present. Another verse confirms this:

بَلْ هُوَ اٰيٰتٌۢ بَيِّنٰتٌ فِيْ صُدُوْرِ الَّذِيْنَ اُوْتُوا الْعِلْمَ [2]

Meaning that, the Holy Quran is composed of clear Signs in the bosoms of those who have been bestowed knowledge.

This verse clearly means that the believers have been bestowed knowledge of the Holy Quran and the ability to act upon it. As the Quran is preserved in the bosoms of the believers, the verse, اِنَّا نَحْنُ نَزَّلْنَا الذِّكْرَ وَ اِنَّا لَهٗ لَحٰفِظُوْنَ[3] cannot have any meaning other than that it will not be obliterated from their bosoms the way the Torah and the Gospels were obliterated from the bosoms of the Jews and Christians; and that although the Torah and the Gospels remained in their hands and safe boxes, they vanished from their hearts. That is to say, their hearts did not remain steadfast upon them and they failed to establish and preserve the Torah and the Gospels in their hearts. In short, this verse proclaims loudly that no part of the teaching of the Holy Quran will go to ruin and

1. The Holy Quran is called *adh-Dhikr* in the above-mentioned verse, *Sūrah al-Ḥijr,* 15:10. [Publisher]

2. *Sūrah al-'Ankabūt,* 29:50 [Publisher]

3. Verily, We Ourself have sent down this Exhortation, and most surely We will be its Guardian (*Sūrah al-Ḥijr,* 15:10). [Publisher]

waste, and that just as it was implanted firmly in the hearts from day one, even so will it continue uninterrupted until doomsday.

SECOND—Just as reason demands that, for the teachings and understanding of Divine Books to endure, it is necessary and appropriate that recipients of revelation and persons equipped with spiritual knowledge, akin to the Prophets, should continue to appear from time to time—similarly, when we study the Quran and reflect upon it deeply, we see that it pronounces loudly and clearly that the perpetual availability of spiritual teachers is part of the divine design. Observe that Allah, the Lord of Glory, has said:

وَ اَمَّا مَا يَنْفَعُ النَّاسَ فَيَمْكُثُ فِي الْاَرْضِ—*Part Number 13*[1]

Meaning, that which benefits people endures in the earth.

Obviously the greatest benefactors of mankind are the Prophets, who strengthen people's faith and benefit the seekers after truth through miracles, prophecies, verities, insights and examples of their own righteousness. It is also obvious that they do not remain upon the earth for a long time, and they leave this mortal realm after a short existence; yet, the purport of this verse cannot contradict this reality. Therefore, with reference to the Prophets, the meaning of the verse would be as follows: the Prophets continue their beneficence by way of reflection; and God Almighty, at the time of every need, raises some servant of His to be their likeness and example by way of *ẓill* [reflection], who—taking on his same colour—becomes the means for their

1. *Sūrah ar-Ra'd,* 13:18 [Publisher]

lasting [spiritual] life. It is in order to preserve this reflective continuation that God Almighty has taught His servants to pray:

اِهۡدِنَا الصِّرَاطَ الۡمُسۡتَقِيۡمَ ۝ صِرَاطَ الَّذِيۡنَ اَنۡعَمۡتَ عَلَيۡهِمۡ [1]

Meaning that, O Allah, guide us along that straight path, which is the path of those servants upon whom You have bestowed Your favours.

And it is clear that the bounty that was bestowed upon the Prophets—which we are enjoined to seek in this prayer—does not consist of *dirhams* and *dinars*. Rather, it embodies divine light, blessings, love, certainty, miracles, heavenly support, acceptance, perfectly complete bounties of cognizance, revelation, and visions. God Almighty enjoined this ummah to pray for this bounty after He had also willed to bestow it. Thus, this verse, too, establishes clearly that God Almighty declares this ummah as the heir to all the Prophets by way of *ẓill,* so that the Prophets always remain in the world by way of *ẓill* and the world may never become devoid of their presence. Not only has Allah taught this prayer, but He has also promised in a verse to bestow it, and that verse is:

وَالَّذِيۡنَ جَاهَدُوۡا فِيۡنَا لَنَهۡدِيَنَّهُمۡ سُبُلَنَا [2]

Meaning that, those people who will strive in Our path—which is the straight path—We will surely guide them along Our ways. It

1. *Sūrah al-Fātiḥah,* 1:6–7 [Publisher]

2. *Sūrah al-'Ankabūt,* 29:70 [Publisher]

is clear that the paths of God Almighty are indeed those that have been disclosed to the Prophets.

Then there are certain other verses that prove that it is indeed the will of the Benevolent God that spiritual teachers, who are the heirs of the Prophets, should always continue to appear. And these verses are:

وَعَدَ اللّٰهُ الَّذِيْنَ اٰمَنُوْا مِنْكُمْ وَعَمِلُوا الصّٰلِحٰتِ لَيَسْتَخْلِفَنَّهُمْ فِي الْاَرْضِ كَمَا اسْتَخْلَفَ الَّذِيْنَ مِنْ قَبْلِهِمْ [1]

وَلَا يَزَالُ الَّذِيْنَ كَفَرُوْا تُصِيْبُهُمْ بِمَا صَنَعُوْا قَارِعَةٌ اَوْ تَحُلُّ قَرِيْبًا مِّنْ دَارِهِمْ حَتّٰى يَاْتِيَ وَعْدُ اللّٰهِ ؕ اِنَّ اللّٰهَ لَا يُخْلِفُ الْمِيْعَادَ—*Part Number 13*[2]

وَمَا كُنَّا مُعَذِّبِيْنَ حَتّٰى نَبْعَثَ رَسُوْلًا [3]

Meaning that, O believers from among the Muhammadan ummah, God Almighty has promised to you that He will also make you successors in the earth, as He made successors among those who were before you. And physical or spiritual calamities shall continue to befall the disbelievers or descend close to their dwellings until the divine promise is fulfilled. Surely Allah does not act contrary to His promise. And We send not punishment till after We have raised a Messenger.

If someone deeply and carefully reflects upon these verses, how can I say that he will not come to understand that God Almighty

1. *Sūrah an-Nūr,* 24:56 [Publisher]
2. *Sūrah ar-Ra'd,* 13:32 [Publisher]
3. *Sūrah Banī Isrā'īl,* 17:16 [Publisher]

has clearly promised an everlasting *Khilāfat* to this ummah. If this *Khilāfat* were not to remain forever, what was the point of describing it as resembling the *Khulafā'* of the Mosaic dispensation.

If the period of the Rightly Guided *Khilāfat* lasted for only thirty years, and then ended forever, then it follows necessarily that God Almighty had never intended to keep the doors of blessings open eternally for this ummah, because the death of a spiritual dispensation necessitates the death of the Faith itself. And such a religion can certainly not be considered to be a living religion whose followers themselves concede that their religion has been dead for 1,300 years and God Almighty did not intend at all for its followers to inherit that light of true life which the Holy Prophet, peace and blessings of Allah be upon him, possessed in his bosom.

It is a pity that those who adhere to this idea do not ponder carefully over the word *'Khalīfah'*—which is understood through [the term] *istikhlāf* [succession]—because *Khalīfah* means 'a successor'; and the successor to a Messenger in its true sense can only be the one who possesses the excellences of a Messenger by way of *ẓill* [reflection]. That is why the Holy Messenger, peace and blessings of Allah be upon him, did not want the word *Khulafā'* applied to tyrants, because the *Khalīfah* is in reality a *ẓill* of the Messenger. And since no human being is immortal, God Almighty so willed that Messengers, who are the best and most honoured of all men, should live by way of *ẓill* until the Day of Judgement. That is indeed why God Almighty initiated *Khilāfat,* so that the world may never be deprived of the blessings of Messengership in any age. Thus, the person who believes that *Khilāfat* lasted for only thirty years, disregards, in his ignorance, the raison d'être for *Khilāfat.* Such a one does not know that God Almighty never intended that—after the death of the Holy Messenger, peace and blessings of Allah be upon him—the blessings of Messengership should endure for only thirty years in the mantle of the *Khulafā',* and then He would not care even if the world came to complete ruin. In fact, in the early days, the *Khulafā'* were needed only to spread the majesty of Islam and not for any other purpose because the light and excellences of Messengership were fresh and blooming and thousands of miracles had recently come down like rain. Had God so willed, it would not have been contrary to His practice and law if, instead of the four *Khulafā',* He would have prolonged the life of the Holy Prophet, peace and blessings of Allah be upon him, by thirty years. After the passing of thirty years, the age of the Holy Prophet, peace and blessings of Allah be upon him, would have been be ninety-three years. And this estimate does not exceed the recorded ages of that time, nor is it contrary to the observable law of nature concerning human life expectancy.

Will sane reason entertain the vile notion about God Almighty that He cared for this ummah for only thirty years and then left it in ignorance forever and did not wish to show it the light that He has always shown to the ummahs of earlier Prophets through the mirror of *Khilāfat?* Certainly not. Moreover, the following verse is categorical witness over the succession of imams:

وَلَقَدْ كَتَبْنَا فِي الزَّبُورِ مِنْ بَعْدِ الذِّكْرِ أَنَّ الْأَرْضَ يَرِثُهَا عِبَادِيَ الصّٰلِحُوْنَ[1]

1. And already have We written in the *Psalms of David,* after the exhortation, that My righteous servants shall inherit the land (*Sūrah al-Anbiyā',* 21:106). [Publisher]

This is because it is clearly declaring that Islamic *Khilāfat* is eternal, for the word يَرِثُهَا [*yarithuhā*—shall inherit it] requires permanency. The reason is that if the last turn belongs to the sinners, then surely they, and not the righteous, would be considered heirs of the earth. For he who comes last is deemed to be the heir to everyone.

Another thing to ponder is that God Almighty made it clear by way of analogy that He would continue to raise *Khulafā'* in this ummah just as He had raised them after Moses. We need to see what God Almighty did after the death of Moses. Did He send *Khulafā'* for only thirty years, or did He extend their period to 1,400 years?

Moreover, in view of the fact that God Almighty bestowed the Holy Prophet, peace and blessings of Allah be upon him, with much greater grace than Moses, as He Himself has said,

وَ كَانَ فَضْلُ اللّٰهِ عَلَيْكَ عَظِيْمًا[1]

And similarly, with regard to this ummah, He said,

كُنْتُمْ خَيْرَ اُمَّةٍ اُخْرِجَتْ لِلنَّاسِ[2]

How could it be possible that in the Mosaic dispensation the period of *Khilāfat* extended to 1,400 years, but in this dispensation it came to an end after just thirty years? Moreover, if this

1. And great is Allah's grace on you (*Sūrah an-Nisā',* 4:114). [Publisher]

2. You are the best people raised for the good of mankind (*Sūrah Āl 'Imrān,* 3:111). [Publisher]

ummah is devoid of the blessings of *Khilāfat* for all times to come, then what is the meaning of the above-mentioned verse: أُخْرِجَتْ لِلنَّاسِ [raised for the good of mankind]. Can someone explain it? There is a famous saying: 'One who himself is lost, how can he lead the way?' Were this ummah destined to be kept blind forever and were this Faith meant to remain dead, then why was it said that you are the best of people and you have been raised for the welfare and guidance of others? Can a blind one lead the blind?

Therefore, O people who call yourselves Muslims! Do consider for God's sake that what this verse means is that spiritual life and inner sight will indeed remain present in you till doomsday, and the followers of other religions will receive light from you. And this spiritual life and inner sight, which has the ability to call the followers of other faiths to the truth, is what is called *Khilāfat* in other words. Why, then, do you say that *Khilāfat* came to an end after just thirty years? اتَّقُوااللّٰہَ۔ اتَّقُوااللّٰہَ۔ اتَّقُوااللّٰہَ۔ [Fear Allah! Fear Allah! Fear Allah!]

Now remember that while there are many verses in the Holy Quran that give glad tidings of permanent *Khilāfat* in this ummah, and the *aḥādīth* on this subject are also in abundance, what has been written above should suffice for those who accept the established truths as a great treasure. And there can be no greater ill will against Islam than to consider it a dead religion whose blessings are limited to the first century alone. Can the Book that opens the door to eternal blessings teach such despondency that the blessings and *Khilāfat* will not appear any more and every thing has been left behind. Prophets cannot come in this ummah; if *Khulafā' Nabī* [Successor Prophets], too, fail to appear from time to time to manifest the marvels of spiritual life, then the spirituality in Islam would come to an end.

How then would such a religion compare with the glory and majesty of the Mosaic dispensation in which thousands of spiritual *Khulafā'* continued to appear for 1,400 years? It is a pity that our critics do not reflect at all that Islam would thus be rendered very inferior in its spirituality and, God forbid, the Prophet, whom we follow, peace and blessings of Allah be upon him, would not prove to be any great Prophet, and the Holy Quran, too, would not prove to be a Book that is powerful in bestowing enlightenment. Moreover, it would be a vain, meaningless, and unsubstantiated claim that this ummah is the best of all the peoples and affords spiritual benefits to others for all times; or that the Holy Quran is most perfect and complete in its merits and effects as compared to other Divine Books, and that the Holy Prophet, peace and blessings of Allah be upon him, is most perfect and complete in his purifying powers and morals. Another great flaw that would ensue is that such Quranic teachings that aim at making man like the Prophets in their spiritual light and excellences would be considered abrogated for good. Because if this ummah were devoid of the ability to exhibit in itself the spiritual excellences of *Khilāfat,* then a teaching that calls upon it to attain to this station would be rendered futile.

In fact, the very question—is Islam now forever a dead religion, in which such people are not born whose marvels are counted as miracles and whose divine inspiration can be counted as revelation—makes one shudder, let alone that a Muslim should hold such a belief. May God guide those who are prisoners of such heretical notions.

Now that it has been proved from the Holy Quran that a lasting *Khilāfat* in this blessed ummah has been established in the same way as, and bearing likeness to, the dispensation of Ḥaḍrat Mūsā, the only semantic difference remaining is that, in the past, Prophets used to appear in support of the Mosaic religion[1], whereas now it is *Muḥaddathīn* who come [in support of Islam]. In the light of this proof, it is incumbent to accept the following as a necessary conclusion: Just as in the latter days of the Mosaic dispensation, a Prophet whose name was 'Īsā appeared at a time when the moral condition of the Jews had deteriorated completely; and they were far removed from true piety, honesty, empathy, unity, and true fear of God; and the whole of their knowledge and thinking was limited to mere oratory and rhetoric; moreover, they had become weak and humiliated in their worldly status, likewise, similar to that Prophet and bearing a likeness to him in this age, a *Muḥaddath* must appear in this ummah when this ummah, too, becomes corrupt, just as the Jews had become corrupt in the time of Ḥaḍrat 'Īsā, peace be upon him.

When we observe closely and analyse with a discerning eyes, it becomes clear and manifest that the age when the like of Ḥaḍrat Masīḥ, peace be upon him, was to come in this ummah, because of the perfect resemblance between the *Khulafā'* of the Mosaic and Muhammadan dispensations, is this very age of ours. This is so because the interval between Ḥaḍrat Mūsā and Ḥaḍrat

1. The original states *dīn-e-'Īswī* [religion of Jesus] instead of *dīn-e-Mūsawī* [religion of Moses]. This appears to be a scribal error, so it has been rendered as 'the Mosaic religion' in the translation. [Publisher]

Masīḥ was about 1,400 years and now, too, it is the fourteenth century after our Prophet, peace and blessings of Allah be upon him. And the ummah of Ḥaḍrat Mūsā had become so corrupt by its fourteenth century that piety and honesty had disappeared completely, and Jewish scholars were engaged in unnecessary controversies and vain disputes. Disobedience and depravity had spread among them, and their worldly status had also fallen considerably. The same is the condition of the [Muslim] ummah in this age. The current state of affairs we see today clearly bear witness that this ummah and its ulema have, in fact, followed in the footsteps of the Jews who lived in the time of Ḥaḍrat Masīḥ, peace be upon him. Not only do they resemble the Jews in becoming devoid of honesty, piety, spirituality, and the capacity to recognize the truth, but in their worldly decline, too, their condition has become the same as it was in that age. Just as the Roman emperors had destroyed the Jewish states, exemplifying the verse,

ضُرِبَتْ عَلَيْهِمُ الذِّلَّةُ وَالْمَسْكَنَةُ[1]

The Jews, finding themselves weak and helpless, were awaiting a Messiah who would come as a king and fight the Romans with the sword, as was promised at the end of the Torah, in the same way, the Muslims of today, mostly and overwhelmingly, can be seen in a state of decline. If there are any Muslim states left, they are so weakened by internal discord, corruption of the ministers and officials,

1. And they were smitten with abasement and destitution (*Sūrah al-Baqarah,* 2:62). [Publisher]

and laziness, indolence, ignorance, cluelessness, depravity, and luxury of the kings, that they also seem to be on the verge of collapse. These people were also waiting, like the Jews, for the Promised Messiah to descend in glory, like that of kings, to support them.

Now, let the eyes that can see, and the hearts that can be just, and the minds that can reflect, ponder over this point and weigh and consider whether the two circumstances are equal or not. Set aside even the prophecies for a while, and just examine it rationally as a research scholar and see whether or not the resemblance between the Muslims of today and the Jews of the time of Ḥaḍrat Masīḥ is the same as one shoe resembling the other. Carefully read the Gospels and reflect whether or not what Ḥaḍrat Masīḥ, peace be upon him, spoke of regarding the rabbis and jurists of the Jews, and how he exposed their dishonesty, can be found in the Muslim clerics of the present time.

Is it not true that like the Jewish jurists, our ulema, too, are engaged day and night in frivolous disputes and are completely devoid of spirituality? They are busy branding others as disbelievers while they themselves do not know what Islam is. They preach things that they themselves do not practice. They adopt the profession of preaching and travel far and wide to earn a livelihood. They make superficial pronouncements lacking any authority to please the people and make unlawful earnings. And in their deceit, deception, and treachery they are no less than the Jews.

The same is the case with worldly people who, in order to acquire material gains, regard every kind of dishonesty and falsehood to be as lawful as mother's milk. As for those who are known as nobles and are holding on to their impoverished states, they are spoiled by licentiousness. Many of them consume alcohol like water and have no aversion to adultery. Fear of God Almighty does not come even close to them during any part of the day or night.

Now study the history of the Jews and see how closely today's Muslims bear resemblance to the Jews of the time of Ḥaḍrat Masīḥ in respect of their worldly and spiritual deterioration. There was a prophecy with respect to the Jews in the Torah that they would not lose their domination until Shiloh comes.[1] Here, 'Shiloh' meant Ḥaḍrat Masīḥ, which is exactly what came to pass when the Roman Empire invaded various states of the Jews shortly before the birth of Ḥaḍrat Masīḥ. And the Jews, like the Muslims of this age, had become weak because of their mutual discord, constant quarrelling, indolence, and ignorance, and their inner state itself was indicating their misfortune; therefore, shortly before the appearance of Ḥaḍrat Masīḥ, the Jews surrendered to the Roman Empire. And because of the resemblance [between the two dispensations], it was necessary that a Shiloh also appear in this ummah who would come at the time of spiritual and worldly decline.

In fact, the Noble Quran has made a similar prophecy about the present age of Muslims which resembles the age of Ḥaḍrat Masīḥ, with respect to the time interval [between respective Prophets], and other features. It says:

1. Shiloh is a figure mentioned in Genesis 49:10 as part of the benediction given by Jacob to his son Judah: The sceptre will not depart from Judah [...] until Shiloh comes.' [Publisher]

مِنۡ کُلِّ حَدَبٍ یَّنۡسِلُوۡنَ[1]

That is, hastening towards Islam from every side, and creating disorder in its land, and occupying its cities and turning its honoured ones into lowly ones.

This verse means that the Christians, who will be the party of Gog and Magog, will advance upon Islamic countries from every height and overcome and dominate them to the point that the Islamic empire shall remain in name only—as is the case today. See the resemblance of events, how the adversity of Islam and the period of decline of the Muslims in both worldly and spiritual affairs has come to correspond with that period of the Jews in which Ḥaḍrat Masīḥ lived. Moreover, note how the Quranic prophecy about the weakness of Islamic empire and the dominance of its opponents coincides with the prophecy of the Torah about the decline of the Israelite state.

Granted, in regards to the coming of *Mujaddidīn,* the prophecy of the Torah and the prophecy of the Quran differ in apparent language. Per the Torah, it will be at the time of the breaking of Israelite power, the waning of their authority, and the decline of their kingdom, when Shiloh will appear. The Quran, however, gives the glad tiding of *nafkh-e-ṣūr* [the blowing of the trumpet] at the time of the decline of Islamic power and the rising of waves of conflict, which signifies the deception of Christian priests. *Nafkh-e-ṣūr* does not mean doomsday, because more than 100 years have already passed since the beginning of the tides of

1. They shall hasten forth from every height (*Sūrah al-Anbiyā',* 21:97). [Publisher]

Christian mischief and yet doomsday has not arrived. Instead, what is meant is that a Mahdi and *Mujaddid* will be sent and a trumpet of guidance shall be blown and the spirit of life will again be breathed into the spiritually dead. This is because *nafkh-e-ṣūr* is not limited to the life and death of the physical body; rather, spiritual life and death always come about through *nafkh-e-ṣūr* as well. And just as *nafkh-e-ṣūr* is used in the Quran to signify the advent of a *Mujaddid* who will break the dominance of Christianity, similarly, 'waves of conflict' is used to signify the same deception that has been referred to as the promised *Dajjāl* [antichrist] in *aḥādīth*.

God Almighty has not mentioned the words 'Promised *Dajjāl*' and 'Promised Messiah' in the Holy Quran in the same way as they have been mentioned in *aḥādīth*. Rather, He has mentioned the machinations of Christians in place of *Dajjāl*.

The verse, مِّنۡ کُلِّ حَدَبٍ یَّنۡسِلُوۡنَ[1] also indicates the same. Similarly, the Holy Quran does not use the term 'Promised Messiah' when mentioning the coming of a *Mujaddid;* however, *nafkh-e-ṣūr* [the blowing of the trumpet] indicates the same and makes known that the Promised Messiah will not appear with material and worldly weapons. Instead, his progress and rise will be due to heavenly proclamations. He will draw people to the truth with the power of wise words and heavenly Signs. This is because he will appear at the time of intellectual disputes, and not at a time of fighting with the sword.

The real truth is that God sends Prophets and *Mujaddidīn*

1. They shall hasten forth from every height (*Sūrah al-Anbiyā',* 21:97). [Publisher]

according to the nature of every mischief. For example, in the time of Ḥaḍrat ʻĪsā, peace be upon him, all power had been taken away from the Jews and nothing remained in their hands besides deception, fraud, and rhetoric. And because of their own misconduct and missteps they themselves became subjugated by the Roman Empire. And the Romans, with regard to their annexation, were not at fault in the least. The same account is given in the Holy Quran regarding the time of the Promised Messiah. For example, the Muslims of India are in such a wretched condition that if a reformer appears among them, they cannot even oppose him with the sword because they do not have any swords. The British have seized the throne of Delhi just as the Roman Empire took away the throne of the Jews, essentially due to the depravity and incompetence of their kings. The British are not to be blamed for this annexation, such that swords be raised against them. In fact, the saying of ازماست کہ برماست [whatever we suffer is the result of our own deeds] fits perfectly in this situation. This is why the *Mujaddid* of this century came in the image of Ḥaḍrat Masīḥ, and due to this strong resemblance, was called the Promised Messiah. And this title is not an undue embellishment; rather, its appropriateness for the current state of affairs demanded the use of this title.

Remember that at one place in the Holy Quran, the word Rusul [Messengers] too points to the Promised Messiah. But the question is why was he not referred to in the Holy Quran by the same title with which he was referred to in *aḥādīth*. The answer is so that readers may not be deceived into thinking that the Promised Messiah mentioned [in the Quran] is actually Ḥaḍrat ʻĪsā, peace be upon him, to whom the Gospel was revealed, or that *'Dajjāl'* refers to some specific mischief-maker. Therefore, God Almighty removed all such doubts in the Glorious Quran. He has done so, first, by clearly and categorically informing of the **death** of Ḥaḍrat 'Īsā, peace be upon him, as is apparent from the following verse,

فَلَمَّا تَوَفَّيْتَنِيْ كُنْتَ اَنْتَ الرَّقِيْبَ عَلَيْهِمْ [1]

Moreover, He declared our Holy Prophet, peace and blessings of Allah be upon him, to be ***Khātamul-Anbiyā'*** [the Seal of the Prophets], as in the following verse:

وَلٰكِنْ رَّسُوْلَ اللّٰهِ وَخَاتَمَ النَّبِيّٖنَ [2]

Moreover, by mentioning many acts of disobedience by the Jews at various places [in the Holy Quran], He pointed out repeatedly that the **later** state of ordinary Muslims and their ulema would be the same. And then He also said that in the Latter Days, **the domination will be that of Christians,** and many kinds of conflicts will spread from their hands. And waves of conflict will rise from all directions and they will race down from every height. That is, they will demonstrate their power, domination, and ascendancy in every way. They will also dominate in material strength and dominion, against which all the other governments and states will

1. But since You did cause me to die, You have been the Watcher over them (*Sūrah al-Mā'idah,* 5:118). [Publisher]
2. But *he is* the Messenger of Allah and the Seal of the Prophets (*Sūrah al-Aḥzāb*, 33:41). [Publisher]

be powerless. They will also enjoy supremacy in the sciences and the arts such that they will invent new branches of each. And they will create new and amazing industries. They will also be dominant in policy making, management, and good administration. Their resolve for worldly enterprises and their pursuit will be high and they will also excel all others and will be exceptional in their labour and efforts for spreading their faith. In the same way, they will excel all other nations in their living standards, trade, and advanced agriculture, and indeed in everything else. This is what is meant by:

مِّنْ كُلِّ حَدَبٍ يَّنْسِلُوْنَ[1]

For, حَدَب [*ḥadab*] means elevated ground and نَسْل [*nasl*] means to excel and run ahead. That is, they will excel all other nations in everything that can be considered prestigious and high. This is the chief sign of the people of Latter Days who are named Gog and Magog. And this is also the sign of the mischievous group of Christian clerics who are called the promised *Dajjāl* [Antichrist]. Since *ḥadab* means elevated ground, it indicates that they will achieve all earthly heights, but will be deprived of spiritual heights. This point establishes that these nations of Gog and Magog are known as such because of their national supremacy. And also among this nation are those people who have taken their efforts in spreading misguidance to the extreme and who came to be called the Great *Dajjāl*. And God Almighty has said that at the height

1. They shall hasten forth from every height (*Sūrah al-Anbiyā'*, 21:97). [Publisher]

of misguidance, the trumpet will be blown and people of all faiths will be assembled together. And after these verses, the mention of Hell is a separate statement as per the characteristic style of the Holy Quran, because it is a common practice of the Holy Quran that on occasions where a matter related to this world is being discussed, mention of the Hereafter is added to it because of some similarity. Those who ponder over the Holy Quran are not unaware of this recurring pattern.

THE THIRD POINT AT ISSUE was what proof is there that the Promised Messiah who has been mentioned at various places in Holy Quran and *aḥādīth* is **this humble one?** In my view, in writing out the arguments for this point, there is no need to be verbose. I have proved in this book that a person from among this ummah must come in the name of Masīḥ, peace be upon him. It is necessary for three reasons:

THE FIRST is that the complete and perfect resemblance between our Holy Prophet, peace and blessings of Allah be upon him, and Ḥaḍrat Mūsā [Moses], peace be upon him, implied by the following verse, كَمَآ اَرْسَلْنَآ اِلٰى فِرْعَوْنَ رَسُوْلًا[1] demands it. The reason is that the verse,

اِنَّآ اَرْسَلْنَآ اِلَيْكُمْ رَسُوْلًا ۙ شَاهِدًا عَلَيْكُمْ كَمَآ اَرْسَلْنَآ اِلٰى فِرْعَوْنَ رَسُوْلًا[2]

1. Even as We sent a Messenger to Pharaoh (*Sūrah al-Muzzammil,* 73:16). [Publisher]

2. Verily, We have sent to you a Messenger, who is a witness over you, even as We sent a Messenger to Pharaoh (*Sūrah al-Muzzammil,* 73: 16). [Publisher]

clearly states that just as Ḥaḍrat Mūsā[as] was a witness over the good and evil deeds of his ummah, so is our Holy Prophet, peace and blessings of Allah be upon him, a witness. But Ḥaḍrat Mūsā's[as] being a permanent witness was not possible except through *khilāfat;* i.e. God Almighty established a series of *Khulafā'* for 1,400 years to fulfil this purpose. They were, in fact, servants of the Torah and appeared in support of the shariah of Ḥaḍrat Mūsā[as] so that God Almighty may perfectly fulfil the purpose of Ḥaḍrat Mūsā[as] being a witness through them and they should be able to bear witness before God Almighty about all Children of Israel on the Day of Judgement. Similarly, Allah the Lord of Glory has made the Holy Prophet, peace and blessings of Allah be upon him, a witness over the whole Muslim ummah and has said,

إِنَّآ أَرْسَلْنَآ إِلَيْكُمْ رَسُولًا ۥ شَاهِدًا عَلَيْكُمْ [1]

and said,

وَجِئْنَا بِكَ عَلَىٰ هَٰٓؤُلَآءِ شَهِيدًا [2]

But it is clear that on the face of it, the Holy Prophet, peace and blessings of Allah be upon him, remained for only twenty-three years in his ummah. Then the question as to how he can be a witness over his ummah forever, has only one answer, and that is

1. Verily, We have sent to you a Messenger, who is a witness over you (*Sūrah al-Muzzammil,* 73:16) [Publisher]

2. And shall bring thee as a witness against these! (*Sūrah an-Nisā',* 4:42) [Publisher]

through *khilāfat.* Meaning that, like Ḥaḍrat Mūsā, peace be upon him, God has appointed for the Holy Prophet, peace and blessings of Allah be upon him, *Khulafā'* until the Day of Judgement and their testimony is considered to be the same as the testimony of the Holy Prophet, peace and blessings of Allah be upon him. And in this way, the meaning of the verse,

إِنَّآ أَرْسَلْنَآ إِلَيْكُمْ رَسُولًا شَاهِدًا عَلَيْكُمْ [1]

is proven correct in every aspect. Therefore, the belief in permanent witness, which is demonstrated firmly by the Quran and is agreed upon by all Muslims, can be proven rationally and factually only when permanence of *khilāfat* is accepted. And this point proves my stance. Ponder over this point!

THE SECOND reason is that the complete and perfect resemblance of the *Khilāfat* of Muhammad, peace and blessings of Allah be upon him, to the Mosaic *Khilāfat* necessitates the coming of the Promised Messiah, as is understandable from the following verse,

وَعَدَ اللّٰهُ الَّذِيْنَ اٰمَنُوْا مِنْكُمْ وَعَمِلُوا الصّٰلِحٰتِ لَيَسْتَخْلِفَنَّهُمْ فِي الْأَرْضِ كَمَا اسْتَخْلَفَ الَّذِيْنَ مِنْ قَبْلِهِمْ [2]

---

1. Verily, We have sent to you a Messenger, who is a witness over you (*Sūrah al-Muzzammil,* 73:16). [Publisher]

2. Allah has promised to those among you who believe and do good works that He will surely make them Successors in the earth, as He made Successors *from among* those who were before them (*Sūrah an-Nūr,* 24:56). [Publisher]

It clearly tells that it is essential that a *Mujaddid* in the name of Ḥaḍrat Masīḥ [Jesus] will appear in the 14th century. This is because the Muhammadan *Khilāfat* and the Mosaic *Khilāfat* can be considered to have complete and perfect resemblance only if their first age and last age have mutual resemblance of the highest level. And the resemblance in the latter age was to be on two accounts: first, the decline in the ummah's condition, weakening of worldly power, and a shift in their integrity, honesty, and piety; and second, the appearance of a *Mujaddid* in that particular age, who would come with the name 'Promised Messiah', and would restore the condition of the faith. As for the first Sign, our Muslim brothers not only accept it, but are also witnessing with their own eyes the deterioration of Muslims and the ascendancy of a foreign nation that thinks of their religion as contemptible and inferior. It is just as the Byzantines, after having overpowered the Jews, thought of the Jews as contemptible and inferior in the time of Ḥaḍrat Masīḥ. They are also witnessing that the spiritual condition of the Muslim ulema and the ordinary people is nothing less than that of the Jews; rather, it appears ten times worse! When we read the verses in the very first part of the Holy Quran about the Jewish rabbis— 'that you admonish others to practice virtue and goodness while you forget yourselves; that you find no fault in mistreating your brothers; and that you indulge in various kinds of greed, immorality, depravity, evil machinations, and deceptions for worldly gains'—the heart speaks out that all these verses are fully applying to most of our *maulawīs.*

While our brothers have themselves accepted the fulfilment of one of the two inseparable Signs in this age, then turning away from other Signs is just like saying, the Sun has risen, but the day has not yet dawned! In any case, a wise and just man cannot help accepting that deliberation upon the Quranic verses proves that the Muhammadan *Khilāfat* must bear complete resemblance with the Mosaic *Khilāfat,* as is clear from the word كَمَا [*kamā*—just as]. If these two dispensations resemble each other completely, then in the Latter Days, a time close to doomsday, a *Khalīfah* like Ḥaḍrat ʿĪsā should appear to complete the argument through spiritual teachings and blessings, and not with the sword. And since Ḥaḍrat Masīḥ appeared 1,400 years after Ḥaḍrat Mūsā, it also has to be accepted that the Promised Messiah must appear in this age because God does not go against His promises.

It should now be seen how many people have claimed to be the Promised Messiah in this age. Suppose, for example, that ten people from among the Muslims claim to be the Promised Messiah in this age, then one of them is definitely truthful and will be the Promised Messiah because the Signs declared by God call for the appearance of a true one. Now consider that out of the 200 million Muslims living in the lands of Syria, Arabia, Iraq, Egypt, India, etc. in these times which according to the Signs given the Holy Quran and Hadith is the age of the **Promised Messiah,** only one person has claimed to be the Promised Messiah. Rejecting this claimant who has appeared at his appointed time, therefore, amounts to the rejection of the prophecy itself.

The coming of the Promised Messiah at the head of the **fourteenth century** is established in the *aḥādīth,* the Holy Quran, and the visions of *Auliyā'* with such proof that **there is no need to write about it.** A righteous one shivers at the rejection of a claim made at its proper time and place. Therefore, the first argument for the **truthfulness** of this humble one is that the time when this claim was made is the very time that was **specified** for the appearance of the Promised Messiah by the Chief of the Messengers, peace and blessings of Allah be upon him, the Noble Quran, and the visions of the *Auliyā'*.

Our Prophet, peace and blessings of Allah be upon him, was declared the Prophet of the Latter Days and 1,300 years have passed since the appearance of the Prophet of Latter Days. Now ponder over the hadith in which the seven steps of the pulpit seen in a dream were interpreted to mean the 7,000 years of this world. **Think carefully** whether or not, according to that hadith, this is the age for the appearance of the Promised Messiah. Moreover, ponder over the hadith, الْآيَاتُ بَعْدَ الْمِأَتَيْنِ [the Signs will appear after 200 years] from which the ulema have inferred that the grand Signs of doomsday will start appearing in the thirteenth century [after Hijra]. If the Signs here stand for minor Signs, then the condition of بَعْدَ الْمِأَتَيْنِ [after 200 years] makes no sense. The appearance of our Prophet, peace and blessings of Allah be upon him, is itself one of the Signs of doomsday. It would, therefore, be contradictory, if this hadith is interpreted to mean that the grand Signs will begin after 200 years, because no sign appeared after 200 years. That is why the ulema have interpreted 200 years to mean 200 years after the first 1,000 years, meaning 1,200 years. The ulema are justified in this interpretation because, without a doubt, many great conflicts have appeared in the thirteenth century and the deception of *Dajjāl* has spread like a storm in this very century. And the spectacle of مِّنْ كُلِّ حَدَبٍ يَّنْسِلُوْنَ[1] was also witnessed in this

1. They shall hasten forth from every height (*Sūrah al-Anbiyā'*, 21:97). [Publisher]

very century as hundreds of Islamic states were ruined and the Christians attained great dominance.

THE THIRD point at issue is that if, indeed, a Promised Messiah was to come in this ummah, then what is the proof of my humble self being the same Messiah? I have just furnished some contextual arguments with regard to this, so there is no need to repeat them. But if the questioner seeks some specific proofs, then he should wait patiently so that God Himself may furnish some proof in support of His servant. The truth of the matter is that rational or textual arguments alone cannot fully substantiate such claims; it is also necessary that heavenly support should establish the blessings of the claimant. And this has been the divine practice vis-à-vis the Prophets, peace be upon them, from ancient times. For example, prophecies were made about our chief and lord, the Holy Prophet, peace and blessings of Allah be upon him, in earlier books well in advance; furthermore, the Holy Prophet, peace and blessings of Allah be upon him, appeared in an age which itself demanded the appearance of a **great Prophet.** However, despite all these things, in order to prove the truth of His true Prophet, God Almighty did not deem earlier prophecies to be sufficient, nor did He regard the other contextual arguments to be complete. Rather, He sent down many heavenly Signs to **testify** to the Immaculate Prophet, so much so that the **truthfulness** of that Noble Prophet was fully established and the light of his truth shone like the Sun.

Likewise, it should be understood that if my humble one is from God Almighty, and is true in his claims, God Almighty will demonstrate my truth with His special succour. And through His special Signs, He will **enlighten** the world that I am from Him and not by my own designs. In the event that I am proven to be true in my claim through heavenly Signs, there can remain no reason for denial, for it is heavenly Signs that have proven **many a great Prophethood** and Messengership and the divine origin of the Scriptures. **Why, then, can the likeness of Messiah not be proven through them?** In short, God will establish my **truthfulness** the way He has been establishing the truthfulness of His true servants.

Consider how many difficulties the Jews faced in accepting the Prophethood of Ḥaḍrat Masīḥ, peace be upon him. It was recorded in the earlier Scriptures that 'Īsā would come as a king, but the Messiah was born poor and destitute. It was written in the earlier Scriptures that with his advent, the Jews would regain power, and the Jews believed that he would wage war against the Roman Empire and re-establish the kingdom of Israel. But the actual events turned out otherwise, and the Jews suffered an even worse plight and debasement.

Moreover, it was written in the earlier Scriptures that the Messiah would not come until Prophet Ilyās [Elijah] returned to the world. Hence, the Jews awaited Ilyās' descent from heaven, but **Elias did not descend.** Nevertheless, Ḥaḍrat 'Īsā, peace be upon him, laid claim to being the Promised Messiah and also proclaimed that it was Prophet Yaḥyā [John the Baptist] who had come as Elias. But the Jews did not take a liking to this interpretation. Instead, they kept on waiting for the descent of Elias, just as the Muslims today are waiting for the descent of Ḥaḍrat 'Īsā. But despite all these hurdles—which were severe indeed—God Almighty did not let His true Prophet remain unrecognised, and established his truth through many Signs. This necessarily led to the conclusion that, ultimately, it was the Promised Messiah who had to be accepted as true.

So, O dear ones! Know for certain that there is only one way in the eternal law of God Almighty to establish the veracity of the truthful. It is that he should prove, with heavenly Signs, that God Almighty is with him and that he is accepted of God. Now, ponder that my claim of being the Promised Messiah is not greater than the **claims** of Ḥaḍrat Mūsā and Ḥaḍrat 'Īsā. Think again as to how these great Prophets were accepted in the world: through heavenly blessings and support, or some other means? Consider, therefore, that there is no alteration or change in God Almighty's eternal practices. If I am not from God and am only an impostor and pretender, then **my end** will not be good and God will destroy me in ignominy and will make me the target of curses and taunts until the end of time. For, there is no graver sin than claiming to have been sent by God while in reality one has not been divinely appointed, and to claim to have been blessed with divine converse, saying, 'His Word descends upon my heart and flows upon my tongue', while God has never **spoken** to him nor have His words ever descended upon his heart nor flowed upon his tongue. أَلَا لَعْنَةُ اللهِ عَلَى الْكَاذِبِيْنَ الَّذِيْنَ يَفْتَرُوْنَ عَلَى اللهِ وَهُمْ فِى الدُّنْيَا وَالْآخِرَةِ مِنَ الْمَخْذُوْلِيْنَ [Beware the curse of Allah is on the liars who lie about God. They are left defeated both in this world and the Hereafter].

If, however, this humble one is from God, and He has sent me, and the words that are revealed to me are from Him, then I will never be wasted nor will I be destroyed. Rather, God will destroy him who confronts me and tries to obstruct my mission. I am surprised that people take exception to my use of the term 'Promised

Messiah' and demand proof for it. Reason does not exclude the possibility that someone should come in the manner of the Messiah in this ummah, which is in the likeness of the Mosaic dispensation. The philosophers, too, endorse the fact that the life of human beings is cyclical. Likewise, it has also been established through divine practice and the laws of nature that some people are born in the image of others; the likes of the righteous are born as well as those of the wicked. Of course, the proof of one's being commissioned by God should be demanded. Such proof encompasses all other proofs.

Think about it. When our Holy Prophet, peace and blessings of Allah be upon him, proclaimed that he was the like of Mūsā and a Messenger of God Almighty, those to whom his Prophethood had been established did not doubt his also being the like of Mūsā. Just as they believed in the Prophethood of the Holy Prophet, peace and blessings of Allah be upon him, so did they believe in his likeness. Hence, the proof of one's being commissioned by God and a true recipient of revelation is the root of all proofs. For example, no one demands of a Prophet to give proof for each and every sentence of the book revealed to him; for, with the substantiation of his Prophethood, all such matters are proven automatically. Dear ones! It is not the case that God wants to **establish a novel law** for me. Ponder over the eternal law of God Almighty and raise your questions accordingly.

Moreover, to this date—11 Rabī'ul-Awwal 1311 AH, corresponding to 22 September 1893 CE and 8 Asauj 1950, the day of Friday—more than 3,000 Signs have been shown at the hand of this humble one, which hundreds of people have witnessed. In fact, thousands of Hindus, Christians, and followers of other opposing religions are witnesses to the fulfilment of some of my prophecies. If you conduct the relevant research, you will find that there are certain Signs that have been witnessed by hundreds of thousands of the opponents of Islam. Even now, those people are alive who witnessed numerous Signs that transcend human powers. Moreover, there are hundreds of such people who were told in advance about the acceptance of prayers, which they later witnessed being fulfilled just as it had been foretold.

There are nearly 16,000 people in India, England, Germany, France, Russia, and Rome—from among the pundits, Jewish jurists, Zoroastrian high priests, Christian clergies, clerics, and bishops—to whom I sent registered letters claiming that Islam is in fact the only true religion in the world, that all other religions have deviated from their divine origin and truth, and that if any of the opponents were in doubt about it, they should come forward to contest with me and stay one year with me so that they may witness the Signs of Islam at my hands. I told them that if I am proven wrong, they may take a penalty from me at the rate of 200 rupees per month for the year. Otherwise, I ask them only to embrace Islam and nothing else. If they so wish, they can have the money deposited in a bank for their satisfaction. But no one came forward.

A wise person should consider that if my humble self did not have such perfect certainty in God Almighty's help as can be attained only after repeated observation and personal experiences, how would it be possible for me to single-handedly confront all the opponents of Islam, namely, those who were the prominent figures of the opposing religions and leaders of their nations in the world. It is evident that a mere mortal can never possess the strength to challenge the whole world on his own. So what was it, if not my perfect certainty and personal experiences that gave this humble one the courage to embark on this challenge? And it was not just done orally, but nearly 2,000 rupees were spent on printing leaflets, which were published in English and Urdu, and in dispatching them throughout India and the countries of Europe by registered post. But no one dared to confront me in a contest. Indeed, it was a Sign in itself that the opponents were awestruck.

You can confirm this by asking any of the present-day priests whether or not he has received a registered letter inviting him to Islam. So, think about it. Can reason suggest that someone who relies only on lying, falsehood, and fabrication can spend thousands of rupees solely on publishing leaflets and dispatching them, and offer a hefty sum to the opponents as prize money in case of their victory. Has anyone, to date, ever read about such an impostor in books, or heard of one or seen one? If so, pray furnish a precedent. Dear friends! Know well that unless God is with someone, he can never demonstrate such steadfastness, valour, and financial generosity. Has anyone ever seen or heard of a present-day *maulawī* who wrote a letter even to a British Assistant Commissioner, inviting him towards Islam?

For my part, not just this but I have also sent announcements and letters—whose receipts are still available—to the English Parliament in London, the Crown Prince of the respected Queen [of England], and Prince Bismarck [of Germany], inviting them to Islam. Published nearly ten years ago, these announcements also recorded that this humble one resembles the Messiah, son of Mary, in his excellences. For anyone who reflects, this is yet another argument in support of my truth. For, if my claim of being the like of the Messiah were only a human enterprise and not based on revelation from God Almighty, then it could not have been possible for me to continuously publish revelations in favour of the claim of being the Promised Messiah for ten, rather twelve, years before making that claim. Every one can understand that as a general rule, man does not possess the foresight to plan so well in advance as to lay the foundation for a work or claim that is to transpire after twelve years. And it is wonder upon wonder that God should give respite to such an 'unjust impostor' for as long as twelve years to date—while the impostor is so intrepid as to plan to make a certain claim after twelve years and lay the foundation for his claim twelve years in advance by claiming to indeed be the like of the Messiah. And he does not do so casually, but rather, he calls himself the like of the Messiah on the basis of his revelations and declares a resemblance in their excellences, and deems himself to be a part of his being. And he does not stop there; rather, twelve years before claiming to be the Promised Messiah, he openly and emphatically publishes in his book (that is, in *Barāhīn-e-Aḥmadiyya*) that God Almighty has named him 'Īsā and has promised to cause him to die a natural death and then raise him to Himself and acquit him of all the allegations of the disbelievers and cause his followers to be dominant over his adversaries until doomsday. God not only gives him respite, but also helps him with Signs based on revelation and gives him a community, while He himself says in the Noble Quran: **I do not help the impostor and he is soon destroyed** and his community is dispersed. Indeed, He said to the Chief of the Messengers that if he had fabricated even an iota, his jugular vein would have been slit.

If it is not true that God very quickly punishes the liar who seeks to deceive people by falsely claiming to be a Prophet, then in such a case, God forbid, the inference regarding the Holy Prophet, peace and blessings of Allah be upon him—that if, God forbid, the Holy Prophet[sas] were an impostor, God would certainly have punished him—cannot hold true either. Now, despite such a long respite and hundreds of Signs and occasions of divine support, while my opponents offered thousands of prayers for chastisement to befall me and despite their crying supplications in their *mubāhalah* [prayer duel] that punishment may overtake me, ultimately they achieved nothing except humiliation and disgrace. Allah the Most Glorious knows that I did not desire divine chastisement for any of my opponents in any *mubāhalah*. I did not even pray for the death of 'Abdul Ḥaqq Ghaznavī, who initiated a *mubāhalah* with me in Amritsar; nevertheless, he wailed and cried to a great extent. My purpose with regard to the *mubāhalah* was and still is that heavenly Signs may be demonstrated publicly in support of this humble one. And it will suffice to disgrace and humiliate my opponent in a *mubāhalah* that God should grant me victory on each and every occasion. In short, all these are Signs of my truth, but only for him who reflects.

It is a pity that I am repeatedly asked what is the proof of my being the Promised Messiah. Such people do not understand as to what was the proof of Ḥaḍrat 'Īsā[as] being the promised one and of our Prophet, peace and blessings of Allah be upon him, being the promised *Khātamun-Nabiyyīn* [Seal of the Prophets].

Was it not simply that God Almighty established their truth with numerous Signs? The Jews, though, did not accept Ḥaḍrat Masīḥ[as] and to this day, they deny that he was the Promised Messiah. But he was proved to be from God through his miracles and Signs.[1☆]

1. ☆ **Footnote:** A man by the name of Hidāyatullāh has published a pamphlet in which he has accused me of denying the miracles of Ḥaḍrat Masīḥ[as]. As part of his assertion, he concludes from some statements in my book *Izālah Auhām* that from the very start I am, God-forbid, a denier of the miracles of Ḥaḍrat Masīḥ, peace be upon him. Let it be clear that such people are mistaken in their views and understanding. I do not deny the miracles of Ḥaḍrat Masīḥ, peace be on him; there is no doubt that he did perform some miracles; however, a study of the Gospel raises certain doubts about them—for instance, the story of the [healing] pool and his own repeated affirmation that he was not a worker of miracles. But we are not concerned with the Gospel; at any rate, the Holy Quran states that he had been granted some Signs. It is, however, a mistake on the part of our unthinking ulema that they attribute certain qualities to him; for instance, that he used to fashion, like the Creator of the universe, the frame of a bird and made it alive by breathing into it so that it flew away; that he revived the dead with the touch of his hand so that they began to walk about; and that he possessed knowledge of the unseen; and that to this day he did not suffer death, but rather, he is present in Heaven in his physical body. If all that is attributed to him were true, then there would be no doubt about his being the creator of the world, knower of the unseen, and reviver of the dead. If, on these premises, a Christian were to argue in favour of his divinity—i.e. on the basis that the existence of the qualities of a thing is proof of the existence of the thing itself—then what answer would the Muslims give to such a claim. It would be an interpolation of the Word of God to assert that these miracles occurred as a result of prayer. For, the Holy Quran does not mention any prayer in connection with the flight of something that was fashioned in the shape of a bird and was breathed into, nor does it state that such a shape became alive in

The most essential demand [put to a claimant] is for proof of his being true and from God, and proof of being the like of someone is then established as a necessary consequence. The fact is that all prevailing circumstances testify that the *Mujaddid* of this century should be the Promised Messiah, because all the Signs that the Holy Book of God ordained with regard to the time of the Promised Messiah have come to pass in this age. Do you not see that the Christian empire is devouring all the dominions of the

---

reality. It is impermissible to add something to the Word of God from oneself. This was the kind of alteration on account of which the Jews were cursed. *Ma'ālimut-Tanzīl* and several other commentaries state only that those shapes flew for a short while and then fell back to earth in the form of clay. As such, we can conclude only that in reality they were indeed just figures made out of clay. And just as toys made of clay 'fly' about by human contrivance, so did they, under the spiritual influence of a Prophet, 'fly'. Otherwise, an affirmation of true creation on his part amounts to a grave mischief and an association of partners with God. The true purport is [manifesting] a miracle, and the flight of a lifeless thing, despite its being lifeless, is a grand miracle. That being said, if the words فَيَكُوْنُ حَيًّا [*fa-yakūnu ḥayyan*—and it became alive] are found in any *qir'at* [recitation] of this verse of the Holy Quran, or there is historical proof that those shapes truly became alive and that they also laid eggs and that many birds from their parentage are in existence today, then proof of this should be furnished. Allah the Exalted states in the Quran that even if the whole world joined together to create a gnat, it would not be able to do so, because in such a case it would become God's partner in creation. It would be equally false to allege that God Almighty had Himself given him permission to create. There is no contradiction in the Word of God: He does not bestow such permission upon anyone. Allah the Exalted did not bestow upon the Chief of the Messengers, peace and blessings of Allah be upon him, permission to create even a fly. Then how could the son of Mary receive such permission? Fear God Almighty, and do not seek to convert metaphor into physical reality. (Author)

world? They have acquired every kind of ascendancy, and represent the fulfilment of:

مِّنْ كُلِّ حَدَبٍ يَّنْسِلُوْنَ[1]

and Islam has reached such a deteriorated state, both in religious and worldly matters, as was the case with the Jews in the time of Ḥaḍrat Masīḥ, peace be upon him. Furthermore, Masīḥ came at a time when it was absolutely inappropriate to raise the sword for religion—the reason being that the Jews had themselves lost their state on account of their own depravity, and as the Roman Empire was not to blame for taking their country, they could not be fought with the sword. The situation these days is identical: the Muslim kings lost their states because of their indulgence in intemperance and worthless pleasures. In fact, they even lost all aptitude to run the state. That is why God Almighty gave their country to the British, who did not persecute anyone after taking the country. They did not stop anyone from offering prayers and fasting, nor did they stop anyone from going for Hajj. Rather, they guaranteed freedom and peace for everyone. Then, despite their being benevolent, how could the Gracious and Merciful God allow for an edict calling for them to be put to the sword. Was the physical sword His only means to spread the Religion—did He not possess a spiritual sword? Moreover, the sword cannot be relied upon to spread the Faith in this era. The British did not force anyone to embrace their religion at the point of a sword, so

1. They shall hasten forth from every height (*Sūrah al-Anbiyā',* 21:97). [Publisher]

that the sword should be met with the sword. In fact, people have perished because of modern philosophy, new naturalism, and the evil thoughts spread by the priests.

The proper response to this is to furnish proof of the divine origin of Islam—not to put people to the sword. That is why God Almighty, finding Muslims in the same condition [as the Jews], sent them a Reformer resembling Ḥaḍrat Masīḥ without sword or spear, and gave him only heavenly weapons to eliminate the deception of the Antichrist. As the numerical value[1] of the letters of the hadith عِيْسٰى عِنْدَ مَنَارَةِ دِمَشْق[2] ['Īsā (will descend) near the minaret of Damascus] is 1,400, so the Promised Messiah came in the beginning of the 14th century. And as the numerical value of the verse,

اٰخَرِيْنَ مِنْهُمْ لَمَّا يَلْحَقُوْا بِهِمْ[3]

is 1,275, accordingly, the [advent of the] Promised Messiah was prepared at that time for the reformation of the people. The Promised Messiah appeared precisely in accordance with the Quranic glad tiding that the trumpet will be blown when the mischief of Christians runs rampant. Receiving revelations, many men of God gave news of his advent prior to its occurrence. Some of them even told his name thirty-two years prior to his arrival

1. Arabic *Abjad* [numerology] assigns set numerical values to every Arabic letter. [Publisher]
2. *Ṣaḥīḥ al-Muslim, Kitābul-Fitan bābu Dhikrid-Dajjāl* [Publisher]
3. And from *among* others from among them who have not yet joined them (*Sūrah al-Jumu'ah,* 62:4). [Publisher]

and proclaimed that he, in fact, would be the Promised Messiah and that the original 'Īsā had passed away. Moreover, many blessed with divine visions declared the 14th century to be the time of the coming of the Promised Messiah and recorded their revelations in this regard. After all this, what more proof can there be with regard to such matters, in which some room must be left for belief in the unseen.

In addition to this, some other grand Signs are expected to appear at the hands of this humble one. For example, the prophecy about Munshi Abdullah Atham of Amritsar is to be fulfilled in fifteen months; the stipulated time thereof has started from 5 June 1893. The prophecy about Pandit Lekhram of Peshawar is another one, which was made in 1893 and is to be fulfilled within a period of six years. Yet another prophecy is about the death of the son-in-law of Mirza Ahmad Baig of Hoshiarpur, a resident of Patti, District Lahore, and eleven months remain from today's date, which is 21 September 1893, for its fulfilment. All these matters—which are absolutely beyond human power—are proof enough for recognizing the truthful from the liar. For, life and death are both the exclusive preserve of God. And until God Almighty completely accepts someone, He does not destroy his opponent because of his prayers, especially at a time when he claims to be from God and presents this miracle of his as proof of his truth.

Hence, prophecies are no ordinary matter, nor a matter that humans can manipulate. Rather, they are the exclusive prerogative of the Glorious God. If one is a seeker after truth, let him wait for the stipulated time of these prophecies. These three prophecies together encompass the three chief nations of India and the Punjab. That is, the first is related to the Muslims, the second to the Hindus, and the third to the Christians. The prophecy relating to Muslims is a grand prophecy, since it comprises the following elements: (1) that Mirza Ahmad Baig of Hoshiarpur will die within the stipulated time of three years; (2) that his son-in-law—the husband of his eldest daughter—will then die in two-and-a-half years; (3) that Mirza Ahmad Baig will not die until the marriage day of his eldest daughter; (4) that his daughter will not die before she marries and becomes a widow and remarries; (5) that this humble one, too, will not die until all these events come to pass; (6) that his daughter will be married to this humble one. Obviously, a mere mortal cannot have control over all these elements.

If even now all these arguments fail to satisfy Miyāń Ata Muhammad, the easy way to decide is that, having read this treatise carefully, he should inform me through a published announcement about his dissatisfaction with regard to these matters, and that he still considers them to be lies and wishes that a Sign be manifested with regard to him. Then, God willing, I will pray about him and I believe firmly that God will not let me suffer defeat against any opponent because I am from Him and have come to renew His Religion by His command. But he should publicly allow me, through an announcement, to publish any revelation that I receive about him.

I am surprised that the Muslims are distressed at the appearance of a *Mujaddid* instead of being happy, and they dislike that God Almighty has commissioned a person to complete the argument in favour of His Religion. I have come to realize that the spiritual condition of most Muslims of the present age has deteriorated extremely and the poison of modern philosophy has completely uprooted their faith. Although their tongues indeed profess Islam, their hearts have deviated far from it. In their estimation, God's Word and His manifestations are laughable.

Miyāń Ata Muhammad suffers from the same condition. I remember when Mr. Abdullah Atham was informed at Amritsar of the prophecy regarding his death, Miyāń Ata Muhammad visited me at my place and narrated a story to me about a doctor who predicted his death within a specified time. The specified period passed without incident, after which he went to the doctor and greeted him. The doctor asked him who he was. He replied that he was the very same Ata Muhammad whose death he had foretold. What he actually wanted to intimate through this story was that all these matters are mere fabrications and futile. But Miyāń Ata Muhammad must remember that his narrating the story about the doctor proves only that he is completely bereft of heavenly light. Undoubtedly, there exists One Being who is called God and who shows heavenly Signs in support of His true Religion, not just in a specific age but whenever the need arises and, thus, reinvigorates the faith of people. The story of the doctor serves only to betray the state of his belief in God. I consider it appropriate to finish this treatise here.

فَالْحَمْدُ لِلّٰهِ اَوَّلًا وَّاٰخِرًا وَّظَاهِرًا وَّبَاطِنًا هُوَ مَوْلَانَا نِعْمَ الْمَوْلٰى وَنِعْمَ النَّصِيْرُ۔

[All Praise belongs to Allah, in the beginning and in the end, openly and secretly. He is our Master, an Excellent Master, and an Excellent Helper.]

THE AUTHOR,

The humble one, Ghulam Ahmad of Qadian

22 September 1893; from Qadian on Friday

FOR THE ATTENTION OF THE GOVERNMENT

This humble one states clearly and concisely that the British government has bestowed favours upon this family since the time of my late, revered father, Mirza Ghulam Murtaḍā, till today. Therefore, gratitude to this esteemed government has made a home in my very veins and sinews, without any constraint. Those services, which he wholeheartedly rendered as a well-wisher of this government can never be separated from the life history of my late father. As permitted by his means and resources, he always served the government in its various circumstances and needs with such sincerity and loyalty as can never be displayed unless one is truly and honestly, from the bottom of one's heart, a well-wisher of someone. During the disturbances of 1857—when the unruly people wreaked havoc in the country by rebelling against their beneficent government—at that time, my honourable father provided the government with fifty horses which he purchased out of his own pocket, and he also arranged fifty horsemen for them. On another occasion, he served the government by providing fourteen horsemen. On account of such devoted services he was well respected by all in this government. Hence, as a mark of respect, he was given a chair in the court of the respected Governor General, and British officials of all ranks would greet him with great respect and affection. He sent my brother to fight some battles simply by way of service to the government, and attained the government's appreciation in every manner. Having enjoyed a good name and reputation throughout his life, he departed this transient world. After his death, Mirza Ghulam Qādir, the elder brother of this humble one, also followed in the footsteps of his deceased father and with his heart and soul occupied himself with sincerely serving the government for as long as he lived. Then he too passed away from this transient abode. I am hopeful that many a British official are still alive who saw my father, and witnessed his sincere services, with their own eyes. One from among them is Mr. Griffin, who has also written a book about the chiefs of the Punjab, and in it he has mentioned my father, too, in most respectful terms.

Now my condition is such that after the death of my aforementioned dear ones and elders, God Almighty has turned my heart away from worldly matters and I desired that my dealing with God Almighty may be by way of perfect sincerity, loyalty, and love. So He filled my heart with His own love, but not because of any effort on my part but out of His grace. I then desired that so far as it is possible for me, I should advance in divine cognizance and love and should discover truthfully as to who God is and how

His pleasure can be attained. I therefore purified my heart of every prejudice and sought with an eye cleansed of every impurity, and implored God Almighty for His help.

Then it was disclosed to me, and God Almighty bestowed insight upon me through His holy revelation, that God is that Being who is Perfect in all His attributes, and that since eternity He continues in the one and same mode and one and same manner. He neither comes into being spontaneously nor is he subject to birth or death. And none who is created and subject to death, has such a relationship with Him, other than that of servitude, that it may be said that such a one is a partner in His divinity. In fact harbouring such a thought is worse than even the rejection of His Being, worse than all human evil deeds, and an evil thought of a most extreme degree.

It is indeed true that amongst His exalted servants those who are named Prophets and Messengers possess the highest ranks. They are without doubt the beloveds of God Almighty, accepted by Him and extremely highly respected. They are completely lost in Him alone and have become His very image; and the majesty of God Almighty is manifested through them. And God resides in them and they reside in God. But despite all this, we cannot really consider any from among them to be God or His son. Indeed, in this dispute, the Muslims are in the right and the Christians in the wrong.

It does not appear, however, that in this age this error will continue to exist among the Christians. The British people are such as God wishes to draw day by day towards ascendancy, prosperity, reasoning, and wisdom. They are also making progress in truth, piety, and justice day by day. And it is as if they are the very fountainhead of modern and ancient knowledge. This is why there is the strong hope that God Almighty will also bestow this wealth upon them as well. In fact, in my opinion, God has already endowed their hearts with it in a very subtle way.

Anyhow, when, for our physical and worldly matters, God Almighty has established a government for us from among these people, and we have witnessed such favours of this government that it is not easy to adequately render thanks for, hence, I assure my esteemed government that I am loyal to, and the well-wisher of this government in exactly the same way that my revered elders were. What do I possess in my hands besides prayer; so I pray that God Almighty may safeguard this government from every evil and put its enemy to flight in disgrace. God Almighty has made it obligatory for us to be thankful to the beneficent government just as we are under obligation to be thankful to Him. Thus, if I do not render thanks to this beneficent government, or nurse some evil intent, it would be as if I had also not rendered thanks to God Almighty. For, being thankful to God Almighty and to a kind government—which God Almighty may have bestowed upon His servants as a blessing—are in reality one and the same thing, and are closely related to each other. Discarding one would certainly entail doing away with the other.

Some imprudent and ignorant people ask **whether or not it is lawful to engage in jihad against this government. It should be borne in mind that this question of theirs is extremely absurd, for how can jihad be waged against the one to whom we are duty-bound and strictly obligated to render thanks for its favours. I tell you most truly that only a wicked and depraved one speaks ill of his benefactor.** Hence, my faith, which I make clear again and again, is that Islam consists of two parts: first, that we should obey God Almighty, and secondly, that we obey the kingdom that has established peace and given us shelter under its protection against the atrocities of the tyrants; and that kingdom is the British Government.

It is true that we have religious differences with the European peoples and we do not at all like to ascribe those things to God Almighty that they have attributed to Him; nevertheless, these religious matters have nothing to do with the relationship between the government and its subjects. God Almighty clearly teaches us to remain thankful and obedient to the sovereign under whose protection we live in peace. Thus, if we rebel against the British Government, it would be tantamount to rebellion against Islam, God, and His Messenger. Under such circumstances, who would be more dishonest than us because we deviated from the law and the shariah of God Almighty.

There is no denying the fact that there are many among the Muslims whose religious prejudice has overpowered their sense of justice and equity, so much so, that in their ignorance, they are awaiting such a bloodthirsty Mahdi as would redden the earth with the blood of his opponents. And not only this, they also think that Ḥaḍrat Masīḥ, peace be upon him, would also descend from the heavens for this very same purpose; namely, to create a river of blood from any Jews and Christians left alive by the Mahdi. But these notions of some Muslims—such as Sheikh Muhammad Husain Batalawi and his followers—are absolutely wrong and in clear contradiction with the Book of Allah.

These fools are bloodthirsty and are totally devoid of any love or sympathy for Allah's creation. But my true and real belief—for which my opponents declare me to be a kafir—is that no one will come in the name of the Mahdi, whereas the Promised Messiah has indeed come; however, no sword shall be wielded [by him], and through peace, and with truth and by love, the world will turn towards *Tauḥīd* [the Oneness of God].

The time draws near, rather it is nigh, when no one on earth shall worship Ram Chandra nor Krishna nor Ḥaḍrat Masīḥ, peace be upon him. The true worshippers will incline towards their True God. And remember, under whichever sovereign's reign we may live in peace, keeping a watchful eye on discharging the rights due to him, actually amounts to fulfilling the rights of God Himself. Moreover, when we obey such a ruler with sincerity of heart, it is as if we are engaged in worship. Can it be the teaching of Islam to ill-treat our benefactor, to set ablaze the one who provides us shelter in a cool shade, and to pelt with stones the one who gives us food? From among men, who could be more wicked than the one who even contemplates doing harm to his benefactor?

The purpose of all this preamble is so that the government may remember that I am truly grateful to it from the bottom of my heart and that I am fully engaged in doing everything beneficial for it that lies within my capabilities. I have heard that because of some differences that he has with me, on certain matters of religious details, a person named Maulawi Abu Saeed **Muhammad Husain,** a resident of Batala, District Gurdaspur, reports out of bitter enmity, utter injustice, and viciousness, completely baseless matters to the government in order to cast doubts on my loyalty. He wishes to misrepresent and conceal beneath lies and fabrications the relationship of sincerity and goodwill that my family has with the government. He, out of sheer enmity and personal jealousy, alleges emphatically that, God forbid, this humble one is not a true well-wisher of the government. This foolish one does not appreciate at all the fact that wicked intrigues and unfounded accusations do not possess any power with which the truth is naturally invested. A single manifestation of the power of truth can smash into pieces a whole mountain of fabrications.

Moreover, the foul odour of perversity and dishonesty that is characteristic of fabrications cannot remain hidden from the God-given sense of smell of the officials. All these falsehoods were of such a nature that they could have been brought before a court of law for compensation for slanderous loss of repute, to put an end to such wickedness; however, I considered it, for the time being, an appropriate action to simply **inform** the esteemed government of this person's fabrications. And it is hoped that with only a minor investigation, the judicious government will be able to assess, analyse, and get to the bottom of his accusations. It is necessary to counter such a mischievous person so that no wicked person dare indulge in such provocative activities in the future. Our wise and just government is not unaware of the fact that it should be incumbent upon anyone who conveys to the government definitive information about any matter, and manifests his conclusive opinion about it, must first also have thoroughly researched this matter. Now this just government, if it so wishes, can take the trouble—for the sake of a family of well-wishers upon whom it has bestowed certificates of appreciation of a high order—to call to account this lying informant for conveying to the government unfounded matters about me through his magazine, *Ishā'atus-Sunnah*.

He **should be asked to provide** the arguments and reasons

on the basis of which he has **accused me of sedition** against the British government. Failing to tender satisfactory proof in this regard, he should be punished as per the law for the sake of expediency and for the reassurance of a truly faithful family. Though such **outbursts** are also found in the writings of my opponents from other religions, such as Padre Imad-ud-Din, but due to their ignorance, religious zeal, and incurable prejudice, they are helpless to some extent. And for these reasons they cannot bring themselves to speak the truth. But this Shaikh **Batalawi** has indeed exceeded the limits. I call upon this just government to compare his writings about me published in *Ishāʿatus-Sunnah* in 1892, 1893 CE, with those published in 1884, so that it comes to know that he is a hypocrite and concealer of the truth and a two-faced man. We know that this intelligent, wise, fair and well-informed government cannot be taken in by such cunning intrigues, and that this far-sighted government **can perceive things** well in advance and believes such biased reports to be the result of petty and shameful jealousy; however, the government does not receive divine revelation, and it is possible that the concerted efforts of **some mischievous ones** may deceive [this government] as any human can be deceived. That is why it was essential for me to write something in this regard.

Now, I quote some excerpts from his **review** of ***Barāhīn-e-Aḥmadiyya,*** published in the 1884 issue of ***Ishāʿatus-Sunnah,* number 6, volume VII,** for the government's perusal so that the wise government **may see for itself** what he previously wrote about me and what he writes now.

The excerpt is as follows:

Rebuttal of Political Criticism

There are very few among my contemporaries who know the life and thoughts of the author of *Barāhīn-e-Aḥmadiyya* as well as I do. The writer has the same domicile as me; moreover, from a young age (when we used to study *Quṭbī* and *Sharḥ Mullā)* he was my schoolmate and since those days, we have been meeting and corresponding on a regular basis. Hence, my saying that I am well aware of his character and thinking cannot be regarded as an exaggeration.

The author has never given a thought to opposing the British government. Not only him, but there is no one in his entire family who entertains such a thought. On the contrary, his revered father, Mirza **Ghulam Murtaza,** proved himself by practical actions to be a devoted, loyal well-wisher to the government in the very midst of the turmoil **(the mutiny of 1857 CE).** During that mutiny, when wicked mischief-makers attacked **Trimmu Ghāt** near Gurdaspur, his revered father—though not a major landlord or chief—arranged for **fifty horses** along with their riders, equipment, and fittings—out of his own pocket and sent them under the command of his beloved son, the late Mirza Ghulam Qādir, to assist the government. The government thanked him for this service and he was also awarded some prize.

Apart from these services, the late Mirza Sahib (father of the author) always enjoyed favours and kindnesses of the government and was honourably offered a chair in the court of the governor. The high officials of the district and *qismat*[1] (i.e. the deputy commissioner and the commissioner), wrote him letters of appreciation from time to time—some of which lie in front of me at this moment. These letters clearly demonstrate that they were written with a heartfelt fervour and can only be written to an exceptional well-wisher and a truly faithful person. During most of their tours, the commissioner and the deputy commissioner, out of courtesy, love, and affection, would visit him at his place. On his death, the respected commissioner, the financial commissioner, and the honourable lieutenant governor wrote letters of condolence and promised to extend care and beneficence to this family in the future. On account of this family prestige as well as an age-old well-wisher, the respected financial commissioner has recently made a special recommendation for Mirza Sultan Ahmad (the son of the author) to be appointed as a *tehsīldār* [revenue sub-collector] and its implementation report has already been issued from the district headquarters. In short, this family has always remained loyal to this government and has been the recipient of its favours since of old. In order to substantiate these **facts** and events, three letters of correspondence from among the ones I have before me are appended here in the footnote, so that, realizing the esteem and prestige this family enjoys with

1. During the time of the Promised Messiah[as], a *qismat* was an administrative unit comprised of two or more districts of a province. [Publisher]

the British government, the jealous ones who are heedless of the consequences of their deeds should refrain from their ill intentions and evil designs; and so that the general Muslim populous may not be deceived into thinking ill of this book and its author, and so he may not be a source of anxiety for them.[1]

1.

Translation of Certificate of J. M. Wilson

To

Mirza Ghulam Murtaza Khan Chief of Qadian.

I have perused your application reminding me of your and your family's past services and rights. I am well aware that since the introduction of the British Govt. you & your family have certainly remained devoted faithful & steady subjects & that your rights are really worthy of regard. In every respect you may rest assured and satisfied that the British Govt. will never forget your family's rights & services which will receive due consideration when a favorable opportunity offers itself.

You must continue to be faithful and devoted subjects as in it lies the satisfaction of the Govt. and your welfare.

11-6-1849 Lahore

The writer of this book (Mirza Ghulam Ahmad), specially on account of his scholarly stature and monastic

---

Translation of Mr. Robert Cast's Certificate

To

Mirza Ghulam Murtaza Khan Chief of Qadian

As you rendered great help in enlisting *sowars* & supplying horses to Govt. in the mutiny of 1857 and maintained loyalty since its beginning up to date and thereby gained the favour of Govt, a *khilat* worth Rs.200/ is presented to you in recognition of good services and as a reward for your loyalty.

Moreover in accordance with the wishes of chief Commissioner as conveyed in his no. 576. d/. 10th August 58 this *parwana* is addressed to you as a token of satisfaction of Govt. for your fidelity and repute.

Translation of Sir Robert Egerton Financial Commr's Mursala d/ 29, June 1876

My dear friend Ghulam Qadir,

I have perused your letter of the 2nd instant & deeply regret the death of your father Mirza Ghulam Murtaza who was a great well wisher and faithful chief of Govt.

In consideration of your family services, I will esteem you with the same respect as that bestowed on your loyal father. I will keep in mind the restoration and welfare of your family when a favourable opportunity occurs.

---

demeanour has never engaged in any such activity. To the contrary, however much well-intentioned support to a government is suitable for scholars and monks to the extent of their capabilities, he has never refrained from providing it. The sword of scholars is their pen and the weapon of the monks is prayer. The writer has never refrained from using these weapons in well-intentioned support of this government. As he has expounded many times in his writings,[1☆] he has also clearly written in this

1. ☆ The following is the **original text** of the author taken from Part 3 and Part 4 of the said book, and presented here in abridged form. In the opening page of Part 3 he says:

The matters which are required of the Muslims for their own betterment—through their own effort and resolve—will become clear upon reflection and deliberation without need of further statements or explanations. However, of these there is one matter which needs to be mentioned, on which the favour and consideration of the British government depends, and that is to clearly impress upon the mind of the Government that the Muslims of India are its loyal subjects. This is because of some ignorant Englishmen, in particular **Dr. Hunter,** who is currently the President of the Education Commission, and has strongly advocated in one of his well-known writings that Muslims, at heart, are not well-wishers of the Government, for they consider it an obligation to wage jihad against the British. Anyone who studies Islamic Shariah impartially will be convinced, on the basis of proofs, that this view of the doctor is absolutely baseless and contrary to the facts. Sadly, however, the deplorable actions of some uncivilized people, and those who are uncouth and foolish [from among the Muslims] support this view. Perhaps the illusion of

book for the publication of which he is occupied day in

---

the doctor has been reinforced by his incidental observations of such occurrences, as some ignorant people do occasionally perpetrate such actions. However, it cannot remain hidden from the view of a research scholar that such people are far and away from being steadfast in the religion of Islam and they are no more Muslims than McLain was a Christian. Obviously, these are their personal actions that are in no way sanctioned by the Shariah. On the other hand, there are thousands of Muslims who have always been well-wishers of, and devoted to, the British government and continue to be so.

In the disturbances of 1857, with the exception of illiterate and wicked people, no decent and well-behaved Muslim, who was educated and well-mannered, took part in these disturbances at all. Rather, in the Punjab even less-privileged Muslims aided the British government beyond their means. As a gesture of goodwill and sincerity, my late father too, in spite of his limited resources, bought fifty horses and presented them, along with fifty strong and well-trained sepoys, to the Government as assistance and thus demonstrated himself to be a well-wisher beyond his straitened circumstances. As for those Muslims who were more privileged they rendered even greater and more remarkable services.

After this digression, I return to my original subject. Though good examples of sincerity and loyalty of Muslims have been observed, yet, unfortunately for the Muslims, the doctor chose to ignore all these demonstrations of loyalty on the part of the Muslims, and did not give the slightest consideration to these faithful services in drawing his conclusions. Hence, it has become incumbent upon our fellow Muslims to take the initiative to express their loyalty to the Government before it can be misled by erroneous views.

The fact is that a clear injunction of the Islamic Shariah, on which all Muslims agree, strictly forbids the raising of the sword against a government under whose protection Muslims lead

and day out—that the British government is a bounty

free and peaceful lives, and to which they are indebted for many favours and whose blessed rule actually facilitates the spread of piety and guidance. It would therefore be a great pity if the Muslim ulema failed to widely publicize this issue with unanimous agreement, thereby allowing uninformed people to make verbal and written attacks which portray their religion as weak and cause undue damage in their worldly affairs.

In the opinion of this humble one, the best course of action would be for the Islamic societies of Lahore, Calcutta, Bombay, etc., to choose some renowned *maulawīs,* with a well-established reputation for their nobility, knowledge, piety, and righteousness, who will in turn invite learned men from far and wide with somewhat of a standing in their local region, to prepare scholarly dissertations clearly prohibiting jihad against the beneficent British government, which is the protector and benefactor of Indian Muslims, citing the dictates of Islamic Law in support of their edicts; then send them, duly bearing their seal, to the aforementioned team of ulema selected for this task. When all such declarations have been received, the collection, which may be named ***Maktūbāt-e-'Ulamā'-e-Hind*** **[Letters from the Ulema of India],** could be printed, with due regard for accuracy, at a quality press. Ten to twenty copies may then be forwarded to the Government, and the rest distributed in different areas of the Punjab and India, especially in the areas of the Frontier.

It is true that some sympathetic Muslims have written in refutation of Dr. Hunter's thoughts, but the refutation by a handful of Muslims cannot be a substitute for a refutation by the whole community, which will be so strong and powerful that all the doctor's writings will cease to have any effect and, at the same time, ignorant Muslims will be educated about the true and pure teachings of their religion. The British government will also be well-informed that the Muslims are pure-hearted and well-wishing

among the bounties of God. This is a magnificent mercy.

---

citizens. Moreover, this book will also serve to admonish and reform the ignorant people of the mountainous region.

In the end, I also consider it incumbent upon myself to express that even though the whole of India ought to regard the British government as a blessing of God Almighty in view of the favours upon its subjects through its governance and peace-fostering wisdom—and they should be grateful to Allah for it as they are grateful for His other blessings—the people of the Punjab, in particular, would be very ungrateful if they did not regard this Government, which is a great sign of Allah's mercy upon them, as a great blessing. They must not forget their pitiful state before the arrival of this Government, and the peace and security that they now enjoy.

This Government is indeed a heavenly blessing for them, for, with its coming, all their woes were removed and all aggression and injustice were brought to an end. It removed all barriers from their path, and granted them freedom, so that today there is nothing to prevent us from performing righteous deeds, or to interfere with our peaceful existence. In fact, God the Benevolent and the Merciful has sent this Government for Muslims as a rain of mercy, due to which the tree of Islam has once again begun to flourish in the Province of the Punjab. In reality, proclaiming the benefits of this Government amounts to professing the favours of God. So evident and well-proven is the freedom enjoyed by the people of this Empire that persecuted Muslims from some other countries gladly migrate to its dominion.

In my view, there is no other country today where, under its benign protection, an admonition can be made openly for the reformation of the Muslims and for the eradication of various innovations that have taken root in their religion, or where it is possible for Muslim ulema to find opportunities to zealously promote

This government is a divine command of a heavenly

their faith, to undertake thorough research using the best of their reason and insight, and to publish literature in favour of the firm religion of Islam in order to conclusively establish its superiority over its opponents. It is this Empire whose equitable support has provided the ulema, after a long time—indeed, as it were, after centuries—the opportunity to fearlessly inform the ignorant people about the pollution of innovations, evils of idolatry and mischief of creature-worship, and to clearly guide them to the right path of their beloved Prophet. Can it be lawful to bear ill-will towards a government under whose shelter all Muslims live in peace and freedom and are able to practice their faith to the full extent and are engaged in its propagation more freely than in any other country. Not at all, it is never ever justified. Nor can a pious and religious person entertain such evil thoughts.

I declare truly that this is the only government in the world under whose protection many services to Islam are done that are entirely impossible in other lands. Visit a Shia country and you will find that they become furious when they hear the preaching of Sunnis; and in countries ruled by Sunnis, Shias fear to express their views. Likewise, the *muqallidīn* are unable to protest in the territories of the *muwaḥḥidīn* and the *muwaḥḥidīn* are unable to protest in the territories of the *muqallidīn,* so much so that even if they see an innovation in religion with their own eyes, they are unable to speak out against it. After all, this is the only government under whose protection each and every sect is free to express its beliefs with peace and comfort. This is something which is of great benefit to the righteous; for how can truth spread in a land where there is no freedom of expression and no tolerance for admonition. Only such a country is suitable for spreading the truth where the righteous can preach freely.

It should also be borne in mind that the objective behind

religious jihad was to establish freedom and to eliminate oppression. Religious jihad was waged against only those countries wherein the lives of preachers were threatened when they preached, where it was absolutely impossible to convey the message peaceably, and where anyone who adopted the true path could not escape the oppression of his people. But the British government is not only free of these faults, it is also most helpful and supportive in the progress of Islam. It is incumbent upon Muslims to appreciate this favour of God and utilize it to strive for their religious progress.*

* The referenced text appears in the 2016 English translation of *Barāhīn-e-Ahmadiyya,* Part III, p. 8–12, and also Ruḥānī Khazā'in, vol. 1, p. 138–142, published in 2019. [Publisher]

In addition to that, he writes in the beginning of Part 4:

Recently, some Muslims objected to the article that I included in Part III [of *Barāhīn-e-Aḥmadiyya*] wherein I wrote about the gratitude we [Muslims] owe to the British government. Some people have also written letters to me about it—and some have used harsh and hard words—questioning why I preferred the British government over other governments. It is apparent, however, that the superiority a government enjoys on account of its decency and good governance cannot be concealed. A virtue remains a virtue in its own right, irrespective of the government in which it is found. اَلْحِكْمَةُ ضَالَّةُ الْمُؤْمِنِ۔ الخ [*A word of* wisdom is the lost property of the believer; *he takes it wherever he finds it*].

One should also bear in mind that it is certainly not the teaching of Islam for Muslims—who enjoy the favours of a government whilst living under its rule, and who earn the livelihood that God has ordained for them under the shadow of its protection in peace and comfort, and who are nurtured by its consistent favours—that they should sting it like a scorpion and utter not a word of gratitude for its magnanimity and kindness.

What our Benevolent God has taught us through His Beloved Prophet is that we should recompense good with even greater good and express gratitude to our benefactor. Whenever we get the opportunity, we are enjoined to reach out to such a government with heartfelt sincerity and utmost sympathy, and to willingly obey it in all that is good and obligatory. Hence, whatever gratitude my humble self expressed for the British government in the article included in Part III was not merely on the basis of my own opinion; rather, I was obliged to express this gratitude in view of the lofty directives that were before me as stipulated by the Holy Quran and *aḥādīth* [sayings] of the Holy Prophet[sas]. Some of our ignorant [Muslim] brothers—on account of their short-sightedness and inherent stinginess—have mistaken their extreme view of theirs to be a part of Islam.

اے جفاکیش نہ عذرست طریق عشاق   ہرزہ بدنام کنی چند نکو نامی را

O cruel one, making excuses is not the way of true lovers;
Without cause, how can you be so derogatory towards those who are known to be righteous?

(*Barāhīn-e-Aḥmadiyya*)**

** The referenced text appears in the 2016 English translation of *Barāhīn-e-Ahmadiyya,* Part IV, p. 6–7, and also Ruḥānī Khazā'in, vol. 1, p. 316, published in 2019. [Publisher]

blessing for the Muslims. The Gracious God has sent this government as a shower of mercy. Fighting and waging jihad against such a government is absolutely prohibited. It is definitely not a principle of Islam that the Muslims living under a government, enjoying its favours, and leading their lives peacefully and comfortably under its protection, and being brought up under its continuous favours, should inflict a painful sting on it like a scorpion. He has many times prayed for this government. The following is his latest prayer published in a leaflet printed at Riaz-e-Hind Press, Amritsar. He intends to publish 20,000 copies of it in India and England.

'The British whose decent, civilized and kind government, by obliging us through their favours and friendly relations, has inspired us to pray with heartfelt fervour for their well-being and comfort so that their fair faces, good looking as they are in this world, may be lit with divine light in the hereafter as well. نَسْئَلُ اللّٰهَ تَعَالَى خَيْرَهُمْ فِي الدُّنْيَا وَالْآخِرَةِ۔ اَللّٰهُمَّ اهْدِهِمْ وَاَيِّدْهُمْ بِرُوْحٍ مِّنْكَ وَاجْعَلْ لَّهُمْ حَظًّا كَثِيْرًا فِيْ دِيْنِكَ...الخ [Hence, we ask God for their well-being in this world as well as in the hereafter. O God! Guide them and help them with a spirit from Yourself and apportion them a great portion of Your faith...]

Despite all this, **accusing** such a person of nursing enmity against the British government and to cast doubt about his book such that it incites against the government: **if not the height of dishonesty and an evil intrigue, then what is it?** The well-wishers of this empire and the followers of Islam must not pay heed to the absurd talk of these jealous people and must not think ill of the author or his book. As for the **government,** we are already satisfied that it will certainly not pay attention to such talk about the author. Rather, it will **admonish** him who reports such things to the government for misreporting on his part.

PRINTED AT PUNJAB PRESS SIALKOT

POSTPONEMENT OF THE JALSA OF 27 DECEMBER 1893 CE

I have to write with regret that I was confronted by such circumstances that made me inclined to postpone the *Jalsa* [convention] this time. And since some people will wonder as to what has caused this *Jalsa* to be deferred, some reasons are written hereunder in brief.

FIRST—the desire and true purpose of the *Jalsa* was that the members of our Community, through repeated meetings [with me], should somehow achieve such a change in themselves that their hearts become fully inclined towards the hereafter, and the fear of God should develop within them; and that they should become for others an example of piety, righteousness, virtue, forbearance, tenderness of heart, mutual love, and brotherhood; and they should develop in themselves humility, hospitality, and integrity, and embrace with zeal the carrying out of religious campaigns. But such an effect was not observed after the first *Jalsa*. Rather, even during the days of the *Jalsa* there were certain complaints that some people were rude and misbehaved with others for their own comfort; in other words, the gathering put them in a trial. Moreover, I find that after the *Jalsa,* no noteworthy, positive, and righteous change has been observed in some members of this Community.

I have experienced this because many people have off and on stayed with me ever since the *Jalsa;* that is, some arrive while others leave. At times, the number of guests reaches the hundreds, and at others, there are fewer guests. But sometimes, in this gathering, due to the lack of accommodation and other required facilities for the stay of guests, exchanges of harsh words—out of selfishness and strained relations—are heard among some guests, just like those travelling by the rail quarrel with one another due to a lack of room. And if some poor fellow comes running, carrying his bag with him, while the train is about to pull out, [those sitting in the train] close the door and push him away, saying, 'There is no room for you'—while room can be made for him, but they demonstrate hard-heartedness. Despite having bought the ticket, the poor fellow runs about here and there carrying his bag with him, but no one takes pity on him. At last, railway employees forcibly have room made for him. Similarly, this *Jalsa,* too, seems to be a cause of corrupting certain moral qualities. Hence, holding this *Jalsa* does not seem expedient unless all the required facilities for the stay of guests are made available and unless God, through His special grace, generates tenderness, sympathy, and a spirit of serving others and bearing hardships in the hearts of our Community members.

It is my heartfelt wish that the new converts should travel to see me only for the sake of God, keep company with me, and return having brought about a change in themselves, for there is no telling when one is going to die. There are benefits for the converts in seeing me. But he alone actually sees me who seeks faith with patience and seeks just faith alone. Hence, the arrival of such pure-intentioned people is always blessed and [these blessings are] not dependent on any particular *Jalsa.* Rather, they can speak with me at other times of their own convenience. This *Jalsa* is indeed not like other worldly fairs that must regularly be held even if there is no need. Holding this *Jalsa* is conditional upon right intention and beneficent results. There is no benefit in holding it without achieving these goals, and every effort in this regard would be pointless. It would be a futile exercise unless experience established and testified that this *Jalsa* has achieved some particular religious objectives and unless it is demonstrated that it has influenced the morals and conduct of people in certain positive ways. Otherwise, holding this *Jalsa* despite knowing that it does not bear good results is tantamount to sin, deviation from the right path, and an abominable innovation. I do not at all wish to gather together my followers like the *pīrs* of the present day only to show off worldly majesty. The ultimate cause towards which I strive is the reformation of people. Yet, if an arrangement or plan does not result in reformation, but leads only to mischief, then from among all people, I am its bitterest enemy.

My brother-in-faith, Respected Ḥaḍrat **Maulawī Nūr-ud-Dīn,** may Allah keep him safe, has time and again told me that most members of our Community have not yet attained any distinct capability in goodness, modesty, piety, righteousness, and mutual love for the sake of God. I fully agree with the opinion of Respected Maulawī Sahib. I have learnt that some members, despite having entered the Community, and taking *bai'at* [the oath of allegiance] with my humble self, and repenting earnestly, are still so hard-hearted that they treat the poor from among the Community like wolves and do not greet them with salutation of *as-salāmu 'alaik* [peace be on you] in good spirit, out of conceit, much less behave courteously and sympathetically towards them. Some of them I see to be so mean and self-centred that they start quarrelling over petty issues out of selfishness, and engage in scuffles and attack each other over minor issues. At times, matters become so bad as to reach the point that they start abusing each other and they develop rancour in their hearts. They argue selfishly over petty issues like eating and drinking. Of course, there are certainly more than 200 pious and upright people in our Community as well, whom God has blessed and who weep when admonished and give preference to the hereafter, and exhortation affects their hearts in wonderful ways. But for now I am speaking only about those with perverted hearts and I exclaim, wondering: O God, what is happening and who are these people around me? Why are their hearts ever inclined towards selfish desires and why does one brother cause trouble for another and seeks to assert superiority over him? I say most truly that a person's faith can certainly not be sound until one prefers the comfort of his brother over that of his own as far as possible.

If a brother of mine sleeps on the floor in front of me, despite being weak and ill, whereas I, being hale and healthy, take possession of the bed so that he may not sit on it, then how pitiable is my condition. And how sorrowful would be my condition if I were not to get up and give the bed to him by way of love and compassion, preferring the floor for myself. If my brother were to be ill and suffering from some pain, then how pitiable would my condition be if in such a situation I would be sleeping comfortably and would not try my best to bring him relief and comfort. And if some brother-in-faith of mine speaks harshly to me out of haughtiness, how pitiful would it be if I, too, wilfully and knowingly, respond to him harshly. I should, on the contrary, patiently bear what he says and earnestly supplicate for him in my daily prayers, crying and weeping, for he is my brother and is spiritually ill. If my brother is naive, or not very learned, or makes a mistake out of naivety, I should not ridicule him or hastily frown at him in anger, or tell others of his shortcomings out of ill intention. All these are ways to destruction and no one can become a true believer unless he is tender-hearted and until he considers himself to be the most lowly in comparison with all others and unless all his haughtiness is far removed. Being a servant of the people is a mark of those destined to lead. And speaking to the poor in a kind manner while bowing humbly is the characteristic of those accepted by God. And responding to mischief with beneficence is the sign of good fortune. And suppressing anger and tolerating harsh words are acts of extreme courage.

But I observe that these qualities are not found in some of the members of my Community. Rather, some are so ill-mannered that if a brother is stubbornly sitting on his bed, the latter seeks to forcibly remove him from it, and if the former refuses to be moved, the latter turns the bed upside down and throws him to the ground.[1☆] Then the former, too, does not hold back and starts

1. ☆ This is only meant as advice for my dear Community from me. There is no other purpose. No one else is permitted to name someone and describe his character. Doing so will result in that person taking the path of sin and discord. (Author)

hurling filthy abuse at him, giving full vent to his rage. Such is the state of affairs that I observe in this gathering. At this, my heart aches and burns and this wish spontaneously develops in my heart that it would be better if I were to live among the savage beasts instead of among these sons of Adam. So with what hope for joy should I gather together people for the *Jalsa?* This is not some show from among the other worldly spectacles. Till now, I know that I am all alone except for a small group of friends numbering slightly more than 200, upon whom there is a special Grace of God. The foremost among them is my bosom friend and beloved companion, Maulawī Ḥakīm Nūr-ud-Dīn, and a few other friends who I know love me only for the sake of Allah Almighty, and look reverentially upon my sayings and exhortations, and strive for the hereafter. Hence, God willing, they are with me in both worlds and I am with them. But how can I consider those to be with me whose hearts are not with me; who do not recognize Him whom I have recognized and do not instil His Majesty in their hearts, and do not think that He watches them while they indulge in ridicule and depravity, and never realize that they are consuming a poison which will certainly result in their death—in fact, they are such as do not wish at all to give up the ways of Satan. Remember well that the one who does not wish to tread upon my path is not of me, and is false in his claim. He does not want to embrace my faith; rather, he prefers his own creed. He is as far from me as the west is from the east. He mistakenly considers me to be with him. I have repeatedly exhorted you to purify your eyes; and make them see spiritually, too, just as they can see physically. The faculty to see physically is found in animals as well, but man can be described as sighted only when he possesses spiritual sight, that is, when he inclines towards virtue after having acquired the ability to distinguish between virtue and sin. Hence, you should seek for your eyes not only the sight which animals also possess, but also true sight. Cast out from your hearts worldly idols because the world is opposed to faith. Soon you shall die and see that only those attain salvation who were free of, and disgusted by worldly pursuits and had pure hearts. I have become tired saying these things again and again, that if these are the state of your affairs, then what exactly is the difference between you and the others? But these hearts are so constituted that they pay no heed and I do not expect these eyes to gain sight except if God so wills. I am indeed disgusted with such people both in this world and in the hereafter.

If I had been alone in some jungle it would have been better than the company of such people who do not see the grandeur of the commandments of God Almighty and do not tremble before His majesty and honour. If a person just verbally declares that he is a Muslim without possessing real virtue—or if a hungry one were simply to utter the word 'bread' with his tongue—of what use would that be? By these methods, neither would the first attain salvation nor the second fill his stomach. Does God Almighty not see the hearts? Does the profound sight of the All-Knowing and All-Wise not reach the deepest recesses of man's constitution?

Hence, O foolish ones, understand well! And O heedless ones, consider carefully that without true purity—of faith and of morals and of deeds—there can be no freedom in any way. And one who, despite remaining impure in every way still considers himself a Muslim, does not deceive God Almighty, but deceives only himself. And what do I have to do with those who do not wholeheartedly endeavour to follow religious injunctions, and do not earnestly place their necks under the holy yoke of the Holy Prophet, peace and blessings of Allah be upon him, and do not adopt righteousness, and do not yearn to renounce evil habits in disgust, nor discard the company of those who ridicule, nor discard impure thoughts, nor inculcate in themselves humanity, civility, patience, and tenderness? On the contrary, they ill treat the poor, push away the helpless, walk arrogantly in the streets, sit haughtily on chairs and consider themselves to be great, while in fact no one is great except the one who considers himself lowly.

Blessed are those who consider themselves most humble and lowly, speak modestly, respect the poor and needy, and treat the helpless with honour, and never ridicule them out of mischief and arrogance. They remember their Gracious Lord and walk with humility on the earth. So I say repeatedly that such are the people for whom salvation has been made ready. One who is not free from the hell of mischief, arrogance, self-conceit, haughtiness, worship of the world, greed, and depravity in this very world will most certainly not be free from them in the hereafter. What should I do and from whence should I produce such words that should affect the hearts of this group of people. O my God! Bestow upon me such words and reveal to me such discourses that should illuminate these hearts with light and remove their poison with their remedial qualities! My entire being throbs with this deep longing that at some point that day should come when I will see in my Community many such people who have in fact forsaken falsehood and have made a sincere pledge with their Lord that they will safeguard themselves against every kind of evil, and will absolutely distance themselves from arrogance, which is the root of all mischief, and will remain fearful of their Lord. But, as of yet, apart from a few select people, I do not see such countenances. Yes, they offer their five daily prayers, but they do not know what prayer is. Unless the heart bows down in prostration, it is vain to expect that physical prostration will avail them anything. Just as the blood and meat of sacrificed animals do not reach God, but only righteousness does, similarly, physical bowing and prostration amount to nothing unless the heart, too, bows, prostrates, and performs *qiyām* [standing position in prayer]. The *qiyām* of the heart is to be established upon the divine injunctions, and the bowing connotes bowing towards Him, and prostration means forsaking one's self for His sake. A hundred pities, nay, a thousand pities that I do not at all see any effect of these things in them. Nevertheless, I supplicate—and I shall go on supplicating as long as I live—and my prayer indeed is that God Almighty may purify the hearts of this Community of mine, may He turn their hearts to Himself by extending the hand of His mercy, and remove all mischief and rancour from their hearts, and bestow upon them true, mutual love. I firmly believe that this prayer will certainly be accepted at some time and God will not let my prayers go to waste. And yes, I also pray that if someone from among my Community is, in God's knowledge and will, eternally wicked, and is not destined ever to attain true purity and righteousness, then O God Almighty, alienate him from me also, as he has turned away from You, and bring in his place someone else who is tender-hearted and whose soul earnestly seeks You. My condition at present is that I fear the one who takes the *bai'at* with me just as one fears a lion, because I do not want that one should be related to me despite remaining a worm of the earth. Hence, the above-stated reason is one of the causes for the postponement of the *Jalsa*.

Secondly, as of now, our arrangements [for accommodation and food] are extremely inadequate and there are only a few sincere and devoted helpers. Moreover, the publication of many books has not yet materialized due to a lack of sincere ones. In such circumstances, neither my sincere friends nor I have the means to organize such a grand *Jalsa* that is attended by hundreds of guests, both noble and ordinary, who stay for days. Also, the poor guests coming from far-off regions have to be provided with traveling expenditures as happened in the last *Jalsa*. Additionally, proper provision of food along with attendant amenities, such as beds, for hundreds of people, and building enough accommodations for their stay that lasts for days is not possible as yet. It is obvious that thousands of rupees are required to finance all these arrangements. It would be a great sin if these arrangements were made by taking out a loan. This would mean disregarding the day-to-day indispensable religious needs, and burdening oneself unnecessarily by taking loans for such expenditures as no one even remembers afterwards. Even though the convention has not been held this year, the guests have still been coming in droves. Since last year, the number of daily guests has exceeded thirty or forty, and at times even 100, most of whom are poor and needy, from far-off regions who also have to be provided with traveling expenditures when they depart; this is a daily practice.

Respected Maulawī Ḥakīm Nūr-ud-Dīn has been devotedly supervising this matter. Many a time he gave, from his own pocket, travelling stipends to those coming from remote places. Some were even given about thirty or forty rupees each; giving two to four rupees is routine. In addition to these expenditures and his previous financial support, he has recently spent about

300 to 400 rupees on various needs of the guests out of personal magnanimity and graciousness. Moreover, he has committed to bearing most of the expenses for the publication of the books, because books are continually being published—though due to certain essential expenditures, our own printing press has yet to be set up. Nevertheless, Respected Maulawī Sahib is engaged devotedly, heart and soul, in these services. Some other friends, too, are serving as per their capacity and means. But for how long can so many expenditures be borne within a rather meagre income? Hence, for these reasons, I consider it appropriate to postpone the *Jalsa* this year. Let us see how God Almighty unfolds His Will in the future. For His Will overrides the decisions of weak mortals. I do not know what is about to transpire, whether the divine Will is in line with what I have written, or whether there is some other decree of providence of which I am not yet aware. وَأُفَوِّضُ أَمْرِيْ إِلَى اللّٰهِ وَأَتَوَكَّلُ عَلَيْهِ هُوَ مَوْلَانَا نِعْمَ الْمَوْلَى وَنِعْمَ النَّصِيْرُ۔ [I entrust my matter to Allah and in Him do I put my trust. He is our Master, He is an Excellent Master and an Excellent Helper.]

The humble one,

Ghulam Ahmad of Qadian

QAṢĪDAH [ODE]

In praise of our Master and Spiritual Guide,
the Promised Messiah, may Allah guard him against all harm

by: The humble servant, Rahmat Ali of Barnawa

ای ذات تو کانِ گوہرِ علم   دانی تو بہائی جوہرِ علم

O the one who is the mine of the pearls of knowledge!
   Only you know the value of the jewels of knowledge.

از علمِ دلِ تو گنجِ بر گنج   و ز خامہ کشادۂ درِ علم

Your heart has become a brimful treasure of knowledge,
   And your pen has opened the door of knowledge.

علمت بذات روح پرور   تو آمدی روحِ پرورِ علم

While knowledge nourishes the soul,
   You have come to nourish the spirit of knowledge!

تو نافہ کشائی پردۂ راز   تو نشر شمیم عنبرِ علم

You have unveiled secrets,
   And spread the fragrance of knowledge.

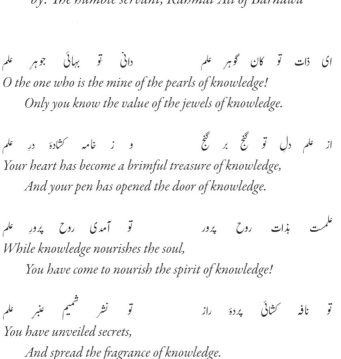

در دیدہ نشین تو مردم آسا   ای صدر نشین و سرورِ علم

The seeing eye finds you the comforter of people are the light of the lamp of the Faith of Ahmad,

O chief of knowledge, who is seated on a high station!

تو نورِ چراغِ دین احمد   تو شمع منار و منبرِ علم

You are the light of the lamp of the Faith of Ahmad,

And you are the light of the minaret and the rostrum of knowledge.

ایمان ز تو جیغہ جیغہَ ابرو   تو غازۂ روئَی دلبرِ علم

O you who is the crown of the head! Because of you, faith has become charming;

You are the beauty of the face of knowledge.

تو مظہرِ آخرین منہم   تو اوّل حرفِ آخرِ علم

You are the manifestation of آخَرِيْنَ مِنْهُمْ *[and there are some others of that group];*

And you are the first and the last word of knowledge.

بر تُست رہِ ہدیٰ نمودن   امروز توئَی چو رہبرِ علم

Only you could show the right path,

Because today you alone are the guide to knowledge.

اکنون تو کلاہ ناز بر کن   ای تاجِ مزین سرِ علم

Wear now the turban of superiority!

O you who is the decorated crown of knowledge!

دادی خبرِ وفاتِ عیسیٰ   کو بود نہان بدفترِ علم

You have given us the news of the death of 'Īsā [Jesus],
Which was previously concealed in the book of knowledge.

فرخندہ بمان کہ تازہ کردی   زیبندہ لباس دربرِ علم

May you always be happy, for you have fulfilled [the promise],
O one clad in the beautiful raiment of knowledge!

آن وعدہ کہ عالمِ زمانہ   کردست بما زِ داورِ علم

The promise which was made by the sage of the all the times [i.e. Holy Prophet[sas]],
That he received from the Arbiter of knowledge [God];

بینم بہ رخت نشان موعود   گو نیست مرا بصائرِ علم

I discern on your blessed face the signs of the Promised One,
Though I am not well versed in academic arguments.

تو مہدی و ہادیٔ زمانی   تو عیسیٰ و خوش پیمبرِ علم

You are the Mahdi [Guided One] and guide of the age,
You are 'Īsā and the cherished emissary of knowledge.

در دست پیٔ گلوی دجال   داری تو کشیدہ خنجرِ علم

Your hand is on the throat of Dajjāl [the Antichrist];
In your hand is drawn the dagger of knowledge.

بر روہمہ عالمان صورت   دارند حجاب اکبرِ علم

The worldly scholars have their faces covered,
With the great veil of 'knowledge'.

آنرا که هدایت ازل هست   آرند کشان کشان برِ علم

You are drawing towards guidance those,
For whom guidance had been ordained since eternity.

برمن نظرے زِ چشم رحمت   ای روئے تو نیک منظرِ علم

Bless me with your glance of mercy
O you whose face is a beautiful spectacle of knowledge!

من تشنه لب و فتاده در ره   تو ساقی آب کوثرِ علم

I am thirsty and have stumbled in my way,
While you are distributing the water of the Kauthar—the heavenly spring—of knowledge!

لِلّٰه تو مکن زِ من دریغی   نوری زِ مه منورِ علم

Do not, for God's sake, hold back,
From me the light of the bright moon of knowledge.

• • • • • • • • • • •

PUBLISHER'S NOTE

Please note that, in the translation that follows, words given in parentheses ( ) are the words of the Promised Messiah[as]. If any explanatory words or phrases are added by the translators for the purpose of clarification, they are put in square brackets [ ]. Footnotes given by the publisher are marked '[Publisher]'.

References to the Holy Quran contain the name of the *sūrah* [i.e. chapter] followed by a chapter:verse citation, e.g. *Sūrah al-Jumu'ah,* 62:4, and count *Bismillāhir-Raḥmānir-Raḥīm* ['In the name of Allah, the Gracious, the Merciful'] as the first verse in every chapter that begins with it.

The following abbreviations have been used:

ṣas *ṣallallāhu 'alaihi wa sallam,* meaning 'peace and blessings of Allah be upon him', is written after the name of the Holy Prophet Muhammad[ṣas].

as *'alaihis-salām,* meaning 'peace be on him', is written after the names of Prophets other than the Holy Prophet Muhammad[ṣas].

ra *raḍiyallāhu 'anhu/'anhā/'anhum,* meaning 'may Allah be pleased with him/her/them', is written after the names of the Companions of the Holy Prophet Muhammad[ṣas] or of the Promised Messiah[as].

rta *raḥmatullāh 'alaih/'alaihā/'alaihim,* meaning 'may Allah shower His mercy upon him/her/them', is written after the names of those deceased pious Muslims who are not Companions of the Holy Prophet Muhammad[ṣas] or of the Promised Messiah[as].

aba *ayyadahullāhu Ta'ālā binaṣrihil-'Azīz,* meaning 'may Allah the Almighty help him with His powerful support', is written after the name of the present head of the Ahmadiyya Muslim Community, Ḥaḍrat Mirza Masroor Ahmad[aba], Khalīfatul-Masīḥ V.

Readers are urged to recite the full salutations when reading the book. In general, we have adopted the following system established by the Royal Asiatic Society for our transliteration.

ا at the beginning of a word, pronounced as *a, i, u* preceded by a very slight aspiration, like *h* in the English word *honour.*

ث *th* – pronounced like *th* in the English word thing.

ح *ḥ* – a guttural aspirate, stronger than *h.*

خ *kh* – pronounced like the Scottish *ch* in *loch.*

ذ *dh* – pronounced like the English *th* in *that.*

ص *ṣ* – strongly articulated *s*.
ض *ḍ* – similar to the English *th* in *this*.
ط *ṭ* – strongly articulated palatal *t*.
ظ *ẓ* – strongly articulated *z*.
ع ʿ – a strong guttural, the pronunciation of which must be learnt by the ear.
غ *gh* – a sound similar to the French *r* in *grasseye*, and to the German *r*. It requires the muscles of the throat to be in the 'gargling' position to pronounce it.
ق *q* – a deep guttural *k* sound.
ء ʾ – a sort of catch in the voice.

Long vowels by:

ā for ـَا or آ (like *a* in *father*).
ī for ـِي or ـٖ (like *ee* in *deep*).
ū for ـُو ـٗ (like *oo* in *root*).

Other vowels by:

ai for ـَي (like *i* in *site*).
au for ـَو (resembling *ou* in *sound*).

The consonants not included in the above list have the same phonetic value as in the principal languages of Europe. As noted above, the single quotation mark ʿ is used for transliterating ع which is distinct from the apostrophe ʾ used for ء.

We have not transliterated some Arabic words which have become part of the English language, e.g. Islam, Quran, Mahdi, jihad, Ramadan, and ummah. The Royal Asiatic Society's rules of transliteration for names of persons, places, and other terms, are not followed throughout the book as many of the names contain non-Arabic characters and carry a local transliteration and pronunciation style.

Acknowledgements

Shakil Ahmad Nasir translated this book from Urdu into English, and Zulfiqar Bhawarna and Saeed-ur-Rahman made important contributions in its revision. The English Translation Section, USA of Additional Wakālat-e-Taṣnīf reviewed and finalized the translation. Al-Ḥāj Munawar Ahmed Saeed, Naveed Malik, Sardar Anees Ahmad, Jaleel Akbar, Waseem Sayed, Abdul Wahab Mirza, and Hassan Khan provided valuable services. May Allah the Exalted reward all of them abundantly.

BIBLICAL AND QURANIC NAMES

Names of Prophets

Adam Ādam

David Dāwūd

Abraham Ibrāhīm

Son of Mary Ibn-e-Maryam

Elijah Ilyās

Jesus 'Īsā

Messiah Masīḥ

Muhammad Muḥammad

Moses Mūsā

John the Baptist Yaḥyā

Solomon Sulaimān

Jacob Ya'qūb

Christ Yasū'

Joseph Yūsuf

GLOSSARY

Aḥad (pl. *Aḥād*), or *Khabr-e-Wāḥid,* refers to those *aḥādīth* that are solitary and not duplicated by others.

Aḥādīth Plural of hadith. Reported statements of the Holy Prophet Muhammad[sas].

Āmīn Lit. may it be so. It is used at the end of a supplication to pray that God may accept it. It is similar in meaning to 'amen'.

Asauj A month in a Hindu calendar.

At-taḥiyyāt Lit. all kind of praise. The name of a supplication offered during the formal Prayer.

Ẓuhr Lit. midday, noon. Refers to the noon Prayer (one of the five daily Prayers in Islam).

Durūd The name of a special prayer that calls down blessings upon the Holy Prophet Muhammad[sas] which is also a part of the formal Prayer.

Farḍ Lit. compulsory or obligatory. Refers to the units of the five daily Prayers that must be performed. Contrast with 'sunnah', 'nafl', etc.

Frontier In British India, 'the Frontier region' referred to the North-western Frontier Province (in present-day Pakistan) and contiguous regions of Afghanistan.

Ḥaḍrat A term of respect used to show honour and reverence for a person of established righteousness and piety. The literal meaning is: His/Her Holiness, Worship, Eminence, etc.

Holy Prophet[sas] A title used exclusively for the Founder of Islam, Ḥaḍrat Muhammad, peace and blessings of Allah be upon him.

Holy Quran The final and perfect Scripture revealed by Allah for the guidance of mankind for all times to come. It was revealed word by word to the Holy Prophet Muḥammad[sas] over a period of twenty-three years.

'Ishā' Lit. evening. Refers to the night Prayer before going to bed (one of the five daily Prayers in Islam).

Khalīfah Caliph/Successor. In Islamic terminology, the word righteous *Khalīfah* is applied to one of the four *Khulafā'* who continued the mission of the Holy Prophet Muḥammad[sas].

Khalīfatul-Masīḥ Ahmadi Muslims refer to a successor of the Promised Messiah[as] as Khalīfatul-Masīḥ. *Khulafā'* is the plural of *Khalīfah*.

Maghrib Refers to the evening Prayer, immediatley after sunset (one of the five daily Prayers in Islam).

Maḥram Close relatives of the opposite sex who have been granted sanctity and thus may not marry one another and are not subject to the requirements of veiling etc. *Non-maḥram* are the class of people from whom Muslims must observe purdah (veiling), lowering of gaze, etc.

Marfū' Applied to those *aḥādīth* whose chain of narrators reaches up to the Holy Prophet[sas] himself.

Muttaṣil Lit. 'Continuous' or 'uninterrupted'. Applied to those *aḥādīth* where there is no break in the chain of narrators.

Muqallidīn Plural of *muqallid,* literally means 'followers' or 'disciples'. The term was originally applied to the followers of one of the four Imams: Abu Hanīfah, Mālik, Shāfi and Ḥanbal. All four of these Imams were true *muwaḥḥidīn,* believers in the Unity of God, who spent their entire lives interpreting the true teachings of Islam.

Muwaḥḥidīn Plural of *muwaḥḥid,* literally meaning a believer in the Unity of God. All Muslims, by virtue of subscribing to the *Kalima-e-Tauḥīd* are *muwaḥḥidīn.* However, the term *muwaḥḥidīn,* has been adopted by some Muslims who consider the Quran and hadith to be sufficient sources of guidance and do not follow any Imam.

Rak'āt Plural of *rak'ah,* which refers to one cycle of the formal Prayer, consisting of standing, bowing, sitting, and prostration.

Ṣaḥīḥ Lit. correct or authentic. A grade applied to *aḥādīth* that are deemed authentic.

Ṣiḥāḥ Sittah The title given to the six authentic books of *aḥādīth,* namely: *Ṣaḥīḥ al-Bukhārī; Ṣaḥīḥ al-Muslim; Sunan an-Nasa'ī, Sunan Abū Dāwūd, Sunan at-Tirmidhī,* and *Sunan Ibni Mājah.*

Ṣirāṭ The name of a narrow bridge over the hellfire that all people will cross on the Day of Judgement; some will enter heaven thereby, whereas others will fall into the fire.

Sunnah In the context of the formal Prayer, refers to those *rak'āt* that the Holy Prophet[sas] offered but are not prescribed as obligatory. Sunnah *rak'āt* are offered regularly by practicing Muslims.

Sūrah A chapter of the Holy Quran.

Tawātur Refers to those *aḥādīth* that are reported from multiple narrators, further increasing their reliability.

INDEX

Index of the Verses of the Holy Quran

Index of Topics